Catalogue of Irish Manuscripts in the University of Wisconsin- Madison

CORNELIUS G. BUTTIMER

School of Celtic Studies
Dublin Institute for Advanced Studies
1989

ISSN 0791-1890
ISBN 1 85500 001 6

Printed by
Leinster Leader Ltd, Naas

CONTENTS

ABBREVIATIONS

BL	British Library
BM Cat.	S. H. O'Grady, R. Flower, (M. Dillon), *Catalogue of Irish manuscripts in the British Museum* I-II, III (London 1926, 1953)
de Brún, *Treoirliosta*	P. de Brún, *Lámhscríbhinní Gaeilge: treoirliosta* (Baile Átha Cliath 1988)
MSS sources	*Manuscript sources for the history of Irish civilization* 1-11 (ed. R. J. Hayes, National Library of Ireland; Boston 1965)
MSS sources suppl.	id., *first supplement 1965-1975* 1-3 (National Library of Ireland; Boston 1979)
NLI	National Library of Ireland
NLI Cat.	N. Ní Shéaghdha, *Catalogue of Irish manuscripts in the National Library of Ireland* i– (Dublin 1961–).
Ó Fiannachta, *Leabharlanna na cléire*	P. Ó Fiannachta, *Clár lámhscríbhinní Gaeilge: leabharlanna na cléire agus mionchnuasaigh* I-II (Baile Átha Cliath 1978-80)
Power, *Place-names*	V. Rev. P. Canon Power, *The place-names of Decies* 2nd ed. (Cork 1952)
RIA	Royal Irish Academy
RIA Cat.	T. F. O'Rahilly, K. Mulchrone et al., *Catalogue of Irish manuscripts in the Royal Irish Academy* fasc. i-xxvii, index I-II (Dublin and London 1926-58); T. Ó Concheanainn, *id.* fasc. xxviii (Dublin 1970)
TCD	Trinity College, Dublin
UCC	University College, Cork
UCG	University College, Galway
UWM	University of Wisconsin-Madison

PREFACE

Libraries in Ireland and Europe come readily to mind when one thinks of Gaelic manuscript repositories. This may not necessarily be the case where centres in the United States and Canada are concerned. Nevertheless, in his paper 'Cnuasaigh de lámhscríbhinní Gaeilge: treoirliosta' in *Studia Hibernica* 7 (1967) 146-81, Professor Pádraig de Brún highlighted the existence of significant holdings in North American institutions also. His recently-published *Lámhscríbhinní Gaeilge: treoirliosta* (Baile Átha Cliath 1988) confirms the importance of the American dimension with the inclusion of interesting new matter discovered in the interval. The set of Wisconsin documents treated here is one such collection. In spite of being relatively abundant, Gaelic manuscript material in the United States and Canada has not been examined to any great extent so far. Opportunities to enlarge our understanding of both the Irish tradition proper and its reception in the New World remain therefore unexploited. The present catalogue seeks to increase awareness of these issues with reference to the manuscripts it investigates, as well as to fulfil the primary task of describing the compilations themselves.

While the account is brief, I am nonetheless indebted to a number of persons for its completion. I learned of the manuscripts from Dr de Brún. I am grateful to him for a number of helpful references incorporated in the Introduction, for his painstaking revision of all aspects of the work's final draft and for supervising its publication. Any remaining errors are the author's, and certainly not the editor's, responsibility. The Dublin Institute for Advanced Studies enabled me to travel to Wisconsin in August 1987 and I was thus in a position to consult the material at first hand in the University of Wisconsin-Madison's Memorial Library, where the manuscripts are housed. It would not have been possible to catalogue the documents in the short time I could make available for the project were it not for the kindness of Dr John Tedeschi, Director of the Department of Rare Books and Special Collections at Memorial Library, and of his staff. I thank Dr Tedeschi both for his gracious hospitality and for permission to publish the findings. A shorter version of the work was originally submitted to the periodical *Celtica*. The journal's editor, Professor Brian Ó Cuív, suggested it might be extended to include indexes, and printed separately. I am greatly obliged to him for this proposal. I thank Elmarie Uí Cheallacháin for her expert help in preparing a typescript of the manuscript descriptions. I finally wish to express my gratitude to Professors Máirtín Ó Murchú, Proinsias Mac Cana and James S. Donnelly, Jr, and also to my wife Noreen, for assistance with various aspects of the project.

C. G. BUTTIMER
Department of Modern Irish
University College
Cork

INTRODUCTION

The manuscripts catalogued here are kept in Memorial Library at the Madison campus of the University of Wisconsin. They are housed in the library's Department of Rare Books and Special Collections.[1] The well-known Celtic scholar Myles Dillon (1900-1972)[2] acquired the nine items on behalf of the university. They are hence entitled the Dillon Collection. In 1937 Dillon was appointed head of the recently-established Department of Celtic at Madison. The Wisconsin State Legislature had set up the department. The move paralleled the creation of chairs in other fields of learning, such as Slavic and Germanic, reflecting the ethnic interests of Wisconsin's population. While the terms of his professorship included the teaching of Irish history, Dillon's main brief lay in the field of Irish language and literature. Since the early decades of this century the University of Wisconsin – Madison library had assembled an extensive holding of works relating to Ireland, but few pertaining directly to the Gaelic tradition.[3] The purchase of the manuscripts as well as the acquisition of a number of printed volumes on Irish and Celtic philology[4] no doubt reflected

---

[1] The standard detailed account of the development of the institution is M. Curti and V. Carsten, *The University of Wisconsin: a history 1848-1925* (Madison, Wisconsin, 1949). More recent general surveys include E. B. Fred, *A University remembers* (Madison, Wisconsin, 1969), and a *History digest*, published as vol. 1971 no. 3 of the *Bulletin of the University of Wisconsin* (February 1971).

[2] The obituary notice by his friend and colleague the late D. A. Binchy, *Irish Times* 23 June 1972, provides a summary account of Dillon's life. For an indication of his contribution to Celtic studies see R. Baumgarten's bibliography of his published works in *Celtica* 11 (1976) 1-14.

[3] The economist Richard T. Ely, who visited Ireland in 1913 to study the transfer of estate ownership, began the systematic acquisition of Irish material. The Wisconsin branch of the Ancient Order of Hibernians supported the development of the holding. For its origin and growth see A. B. Cronin and S. E. Horsley, *The Irish collection of books and paintings at the University of Wisconsin* (Madison, Wisconsin, 1915). Memorial Library also houses a large amount of Irish cartographic material, dating from the seventeenth century.

[4] Many items came from the library of the scholar J. G. O'Keeffe, then recently deceased. Necrologies of O'Keeffe may be found in *Études Celtiques* 3 (1938) 213 and *Ir. Book Lover* 26 (1938) 26-9. See also below, note 13.

Dillon's desire to strengthen resources in the area of his professional and personal concern.[5]

ACQUISITION

The documents in question were bought from Miss Anna O'Byrne of 51 Hamilton Place, New York. The Rare Book Department's Collection Files contain three items dealing with the transaction. They are: (1) a letter from Miss O'Byrne to Myles Dillon, dated 23 May 1938, describing the available manuscript material (hereafter Correspondence); (2) a requisition, dated 1 October 1938, ordering documents from Miss O'Byrne; (3) a Purchase Order of the University of Wisconsin, dated 13 October 1938, recording prices paid for documents acquired from Miss O'Byrne, together with the date of receipt of the material, 4 November 1938 (hereafter Purchase Order). The evidence of items 1 and 3 in particular, together with entries in the manuscripts themselves and the testimony of the cultural background to which they belong, will now be considered. This information allows us to present an outline sketch of the former ownership and provenance of the codices.

It seems that the lady's father, rather than Miss O'Byrne herself, was the original collector of the material. The father's signature, Michael O'Byrne or in its Irish form Micheál Ó Broin, occurs in MSS 178 and 182 below. Annotations in a hand resembling his are found in MSS 176, 177 and 180. Clippings from the *New York Times* newspaper, used as bookmarks, appear in MSS 175 and 177, and are either dated or contain entries for the years 1915-16. These manuscripts are thus readily linked with O'Byrne, as on the evidence of MS 178 he was a New York resident, and had been acquiring Gaelic matter since 1905 at least. He may also have been familiar with the circle of Irish-language scholars and enthusiasts active in

---

[5] Dillon resigned his UWM post in 1946, and subsequently taught at Chicago and Edinburgh. He was Senior Professor in the School of Celtic Studies of the Dublin Institute for Advanced Studies from 1949 until his death. While his stay at Madison was comparatively short, Dillon nonetheless trained in Celtic philology a number of students who subsequently became prominent in various areas of scholarship in the United States, figures like Morton Bloomfield, William Heist and W. P. Lehmann.

New York at the turn of the century.[6] The name of a member of the *cénacle*, Dáithí Ua Caoimh of South Brooklyn, occurs as former owner in MS 178. He is to be identified with the scribe Dáibhí Ó Caoimh whose works served as exemplars for other manuscripts compiled in New York in the years 1894-1912.[7] Apart from contacts of this nature, information furnished by Miss O'Byrne suggests how her father might otherwise have developed and sustained his interest. In her 1938 Correspondence she stated to Dillon that Michael O'Byrne acted as treasurer of the Irish Industries Depot in New York until about 1923. The latter enterprise was located in Manhattan at 780 Lexington Avenue. It sold items of Irish manufacture such as woollens, and also functioned as a clearing-house for Gaelic texts and books on Ireland.[8] O'Byrne's involvement with the store must have facilitated his obtaining manuscripts. There is admittedly no direct testimony either in the Madison archives or the volumes themselves to confirm that any of the works catalogued here was acquired in this way.

The Collection Files records discussed thus far do not indicate how Miss O'Byrne came into contact with Dillon. In this regard, I believe the following point might be considered. Many Americans in the fields of Irish and Celtic studies dealt with the Depot. Among the latter was Fred Norris Robinson (1871-1966) of Harvard, the single most influential Celticist in the United States in his time.[9]

---

[6] For this circle and its activities see P. Mac Aonghusa, 'An Ghaeilge i Meiriceá'; B. Ó Buachalla, *'An Gaodhal* i Meiriceá'; L. Ó Dochartaigh, 'Nótaí ar Ghluaiseacht na Gaeilge i Meiriceá, 1872-1891'; and B. Ó Conaire, 'Pádraig Ó Beirn: fear a d'fhill': all in S. Ó hAnnracháin (ed.), *Go Meiriceá siar* ([Baile Átha Cliath] 1979) 13-20, 38-56, 65-90, 111-24, respectively.

[7] Dáibhí Ó Caoimh provided Tomás D. de Norradh with one of the two sources used in the compilation of NLI MS G 341, a copy of the saga Cath Fionntrágha, written in New York in the years 1890-94 (see *NLI Cat.* viii (1984) 16-18). Another Ó Caoimh manuscript, completed in 1880, served as the source of Ferriter MS 17, a collection of tales, copied by Pádraig Feiritéar (1856-1924) in New York in 1912 (MS 17, p. 7: 'Is i Siegel Park ann san Bhronx atáim ag obair anois, ⁊ i'm' chómhnaidhe i [?200 *cancelled*] 201 E. 42 St. N.Y. P. Feirritéar'). Ferriter MS 33, an anthology of Munster poetry in Irish, was compiled by Ó Caoimh between 1859 and 1862. For the Ferriter manuscript collection, now in University College, Dublin, see de Brún, *Treoirliosta*, 2-3 § 7/2. Ferriter's career is sketched by S. Ó Sé in *Kerry Arch. and Hist. Soc. Jn.* 3 (1970) 116-30.

[8] I hope to account for other manuscripts previously associated with the Depot in the Introduction to *Catalogue of Irish manuscripts in Houghton Library, Harvard University*, which is in preparation.

[9] For a review of Robinson's life see E. P. Hamp, *Lochlann* 4 (1969) 309-312.

Correspondence with the entrepôt relating to the purchase of books and the acquisition of certain of Harvard's Gaelic codices survives in Robinson's personal papers.[10] Among these papers there are letters from Dillon to Robinson which indicate that an amicable contact based on mutual academic interest existed between the two since the mid 1930s, if not earlier.[11] Robinson firmly endorsed Dillon's candidature for the Madison chair.[12] In a further attempt to support him in practical matters, the Harvard scholar may have drawn the Irishman's attention to the importance of the Industries Depot and its network of connections for the formation of a Gaelic library in Wisconsin. Other senior academics, such as R. I. Best (1872-1959), director of the National Library of Ireland, displayed a similar avuncular concern for Dillon at the outset of his career in the mid-West. Best hoped to supply Dillon with complete sets of the periodicals *Revue Celtique* and *Zeitschrift für celtische Philologie* to start up a specialist Celtic holding at Madison.[13]

Miss O'Byrne's letter to Dillon mentions eight items as being available for purchase. Her account of the material, followed by suggested identification of the documents with manuscripts in the present collection may be set out thus:

---

[10] Harvard University Archives (Pusey Library, Harvard) HUG (FP) 40.10-50. The collection comprises some 13 boxes; correspondence with the Depot is in HUG (FP) 40.10 box 3.

[11] HUG (FP) 40.10 box 3, 40.15 box 4 etc.

[12] Robinson's support is mentioned in the *Madison Wisconsin State Journal*'s account, dated 25 August 1937, of Dillon's appointment to the Celtic position.

[13] Best to Fred Norris Robinson recommending Dillon for the Wisconsin professorship (HUG (FP) 40.10 box 3). Best may perhaps have drawn Dillon's attention to the availability of J. G. O'Keeffe's personal library after the latter's death in 1938. For obituary notices outlining Best's own career see R. Baumgarten, *Bibliography of Irish linguistics and literature* (Dublin 1986) 14-15 §§ 178-86.

	Correspondence	Catalogue no.
1	'Irish Grammar Manuscript, 1603.'	179
2	'Manuscript by Labhrás Ó Fuarthain, 1782.'	177
3	'Manuscript: Battle of Clontarf etc. 1832.'	178
4	'Manuscript: Battle of Clontarf.'	175
5	'Manuscript: Trí Bior-gaithe an Bhais 1851.'	176
6	'Manuscript Catechism by Richard Power 1860.'	182
7	'Manuscript written 1724.'	?
8	'another delapidated manuscript.'	181 (?)

The Purchase Order of the University of Wisconsin lists seven items bought from Miss O'Byrne. The titles, prices and suggested identifications are as follows:

	Manuscript	Cost ($)	Catalogue no.
1	'Three Shafts'	5.00	176
2	'17th century'	7.50	179
3	'O'Donovan Rossa'	10.00	183
4	'Small Octavo poems'	10.00	180
5	'Clontarf'	15.00	175
6	'Ulster Stories'	15.00	178
7	'Horan 1762'	15.00	177

Of the present collection, therefore, only MS 181 is not overtly accounted for in either enumeration. For reasons to be discussed below, it can be argued with some plausibility that it must be included with the O'Byrne material, possibly as entry 8 in Miss O'Byrne's Correspondence list. Entry 7 in the latter source, the 'Manuscript written 1724', is problematical. None of the nine documents described here carries this date. One might suggest that because Miss O'Byrne's catalogue is incomplete, as a comparison with the Purchase Order shows, entry 7 is an error. Against this, however, is the fact that the vendor's characterization of the manuscripts she describes, though brief, is by and large accurate. The Purchase Order itself, of course, is not a true reflection of the items acquired. Nevertheless it is unlikely that Dillon or the university would have neglected to buy a document earlier in date than the majority of the other compilations obtained.[14] Thus the question of whether the 'Manuscript written 1724' is genuine must remain open.

PROVENANCE

Waterford: There appears to be no separate purchase order or alternative statement of donation for MS 181 in the Madison records. Added to this negative consideration, a more positive piece of internal evidence in the volume provides a likely connection between it and certain other O'Byrne documents. A note at the conclusion of the text ascribes the work to the Rev. John Meany, parish priest of Kilrossanty in the Co. Waterford barony of Decies-without-Drum.[15] The manuscript's provenance is significant in that MSS 177 and 182, and perhaps also MS 176, originated in the same county. These associations are reviewed in what follows, both to clarify the nature of the O'Byrne collection *per se*, and as a sidelight on Waterford's rich, though relatively unexplored scribal heritage.

In 1835 the Waterford Gaelic enthusiast Philip Barron[16] provided a brief account of Fr Meany. He described him as

> an eminent classical scholar. He read and wrote his native language; and to this accidental circumstance we are indebted for possessing, at this day, those compositions which will be so highly prized, when they go before the public. This exception but the more forcibly proves the loss which has been sustained, in consequence of Irish divines not being able generally to write the language in which their sermons are preached.

---

[14] The date of MS 179 is problematical: see the discussion below for details.

[15] For Kilrossanty parish see Power, *Place-names*, 148-57.

[16] For information on Barron's life and his involvement with the Irish language see M. Butler, 'Philip Barron', *Catholic Record of Waterford and Lismore* March 1916 – Feb. 1918; D. Ryan, *The Sword of Light* (London 1939) 111-152 (based largely on Butler's biography); cf. also N. Ní Shéaghdha, *Collectors of Irish manuscripts: motives and methods* (Dublin 1985) 16-17.

Barron made these observations when Fr Meany's 'Sermon on Charity', the text represented in MS 181, was published as part of a project to rescue the Irish language from oblivion.[17] In view of only slight orthographic differences between it and this printed version, MS 181 may well have been Barron's source. The same homily was again published in 1889, when an approximate date of its original composition was also furnished. On the occasion of its second printing, the sermon was stated to have been 'spoken about 80 years since by Father John Meany, P.P. of Kilrossanty'. Mr [Patrick] Carmody of Comeragh Mills transcribed it from a manuscript in the possession of Fr Michael Casey, PP, successor to Fr Meany in the parish.[18] That the latter manuscript is not MS 181 of the present collection may perhaps be inferred from orthographic differences between the printed text and our document.

The survival of other homiletic matter which can be associated with the priest confirms Barron's description of Fr Meany as an active preacher in Gaelic. Fr Meany can be identified by handwriting with Seán Ó Maonaigh, scribe of section (b) of RIA MS 3 C 3.[19] This document, a collection of sermons, was written in Kilrossanty as well. A copy of Meany's homily on family life occurs in NLI MS G 403 (pp. 310-20).[20] The latter compilation also includes (pp. 1-6) the poem *Mo chreach ghéar féin ┐ mo dheacair / an uair thángas féin aréir go dtí'd gheata*, a lament for the priest. The form of the elegy echoes the traditional keen. It is perhaps interesting to note that elsewhere in Ireland in pre-Famine times the keen and activities related to it in particular were the object of much clerical hostility.[21] One wonders whether the lament represents the Gaelic world's reciprocation of Fr Meany's identification with native culture. There is finally a possibility that Fr John Meany was related to the Rev. P.

[17] The work was printed by John S. Folds in *Irish sermons with translations* (Dublin 1835) on Barron's behalf, with the latter's remarks on Fr Meany occurring in prefatory matter on pp. v-vi. Séamus Ua Casaide's article on Meany in the *Waterford and S.E. Ire. Arch. Soc. Jn.* 14 (1911) 193 repeats Barron's account.
[18] *Gaelic Journal* 4 (1889) 4-6, 19-22. This edition includes an explanatory glossary. Information on date and source of homily on p. 4.
[19] See *RIA Cat.*, 2899-2903.
[20] See *NLI Cat.* ix (1986) 45-9 for a description of the manuscript.
[21] S. Ó Coileáin, 'The Irish lament: an oral genre', *Studia Hibernica* 24 (1984-8) 97-117, especially pp. 115 ff., contains a recent treatment of this issue.

Meany of Lismore, Co. Waterford, scribe of NLI MS G 1125, a
volume of sermons in Irish written about 1845.[22]

Manuscript 177 is the work of the copyist Labhrás Ó Fuartháin,
to whom at least five other compilations are attributed either in
whole or in part.[23] These manuscripts, containing a mixture of
religious and secular matter such as historic tales and contemporary
verse, indicate that his scribal activity in the years 1768-86 was
centered on Portlaw in the north Waterford barony of Upperthird.[24]
Manuscript 177 shows that his early associations were with Baile Uí
Chnáimhín, probably to be identified with Ballynevin townland in
Mothel parish in the same barony.[25] In 1859 the famous Waterford-
born scholar John O Daly (*ob.* 1878) edited the Fianaíocht text
Agallamh Oisín agus Phádraig from one of Ó Fuartháin's
compilations, now UCC Ir. MS 96 (pp. 75-89).[26] In the introduction
to the work, O Daly claimed that the scribe 'kept a village school at
Killeen near Portlaw' (p. xxxi). A recent study places Ó Fuartháin in
the context of the vigorous scribal tradition found in the contiguous
areas of south Tipperary, south Kilkenny and north Waterford at the
turn of the eighteenth century.[27] Section (b) of MS 177 and NLI MS

---

[22] For a brief notice of the document see *MSS sources suppl.* 1, 480.

[23] *MSS sources* 3, 643, provides a summary account of this material; see further
RIA Cat., 2127-9 (23 Q 8), and for manuscripts in St John's College, Waterford, Ó
Fiannachta, *Leabharlanna na cléire* I, 10-11 (MS 8), 34-5 (MS 28).
    When discussing the story 'The adventures of Torolbh MacStairn's three sons',
Douglas Hyde refers to 'a voluminous MS. of some 600 closely written pages, bound
in sheepskin, made by Laurence Foran of Waterford, in 1812, given me by Mr. W.
Doherty, C.E.', in *Beside the fire: a collection of Irish Gaelic folk stories* (London
1910) xxxiii n. 2. The only Ó Fuartháin manuscript currently in the UCG Hyde
collection is no. 18, a miscellany of tales and poetry, written in Portlaw in 1786, but
it does not contain a copy of the saga Hyde mentions. Hyde may have been thinking
of MS 21, an anthology of Ossianic and other poetry, romantic tales and other prose,
compiled mainly by M. O Forranán (Ml. Foren) in the years 1811-12 (see *MSS
sources* 3, 643). Manuscript 21 is no longer part of the Hyde collection. For its
present whereabouts see de Brún, *Treoirliosta*, 37 § 132; and *ibid.*, 20 § 62/1, for a
general account of the Hyde material.

[24] For this location see Power, *Place-names*, 388-9.

[25] *ibid.*, 404.

[26] Ossianic Soc. Trans. IV (1859 for 1856) 1-63; Prof. Pádraig Ó Fiannachta
discusses the composition in 'The development of the debate between Pádraig and
Oisín', *Béaloideas* 54-5 (1986-7) 183-205, especially pp. 195 ff. The manuscript will
be described in B. Ó Conchúir, *Clár lámhscríbhinní Gaeilge Choláiste Ollscoile
Chorcaí: cnuasach an Phaoraigh agus cnuasaigh eile*, in preparation as the next
volume of the catalogue mentioned in note 39 below.

[27] E. Ó Néill, *Gleann an Óir* (Baile Átha Cliath 1988) 106.

G 311 appear originally to have been portions of the same document, with one manuscript supplementing the other at points where gaps occur in either.[28] G 311 confirms Ó Fuartháin's previous links with Ballynevin.

Manuscript 182 is the work of Riocard Paor. The years 1850-67 seem to have been the productive period of his life, a fact indicated by the survival of eleven other compilations from that time.[29] Religious material predominates in these documents, including copies of well-known tracts like *Trompa na bhFlaitheas* and *Stiúrthóir an Pheacaigh*. The bulk of his output was apparently produced in Waterford city, and it is likely that MS 182 was also written there.

Manuscript 176 does not have a scribal signature, but the work is to be attributed to Tomás Ó hIceadha (1775-1856), on the basis of his distinctive, somewhat crabbed penmanship.[30] Over thirty manuscripts from this prolific copyist are extant, dating from 1817 until well after the Famine. Many of these also contain devotional matter such as missals, sermons, and saints' lives.[31] Ó hIceadha was a native of Graystown near Killenaule, Co. Tipperary. A number of his surviving productions are associated with this location,[32] as well

---

[28] For G 311 see *NLI Cat.* vii (1982) 38-42. G 311 begins (p. 95) with a copy of Ó Cléirigh's *Sanasán nua* at the point where MS 177 (b)'s version of the text ends (with p. 94). MS 177 (b) continues (p. 277) with *Eachtra an Mhadra Mhaoil* at the point G 311's copy of the work breaks off (p. 276).

[29] For Paor's output see *MSS sources* 4, 9; see further *RIA Cat.* 305 (23 L 5). and for items in St John's College, Waterford, Ó Fiannachta, *Leabharlanna na cléire* I, 12-13, 16, 32-3, 38-40 (MSS 10, 13, 26, 30).

[30] His script is described in similar terms in Ó Fiannachta, *Leabharlanna na cléire* I, 2.

[31] See *Mss sources* 3, 664; see further *RIA Cat.*, 381-3 (24 L 19), 388-9 (24 L 33), 391-4 (24 L 24), 525-6 (23 D 26), 2448-50 (24 L 26), 2530-34 (24 L 27); *NLI Cat.* vi (1980) 26-30 (G 230), vii (1982) 91-3 (G 329); *Éigse* 17 (1978) 383-4; UCG Hyde MS 24 (compiled *c.* 1827 [p. 101]; not included in *MSS sources*) and the items cited in notes 32-7 below.

[32] See for instance P. Ó Fiannachta, *Lámhscríbhinní Gaeilge Choláiste Phádraig, Má Nuad: clár* IV (Má Nuad 1967) 27-8 (M 108); *NLI Cat.* ix (1986) 60-61 (G 415) etc.

as with other areas in the same county like Ardfinnan.[33] In addition
to his connection with Tipperary, the scribe's ties with Waterford
are a dominant strand in his *oeuvre*.[34] Ó hIceadha compiled a mass
book for a patron in Kilrossanty in 1824.[35] No fewer than six of his
manuscripts were written in the 1830s and 1840s for Fr Dominic
O'Brien, afterwards Catholic bishop of Waterford and Lismore in
the years 1855-73.[36] The latter documents were completed in
Waterford city, principally at the diocesan seminary, St John's
College, where thirteen of Ó hIceadha's manuscripts are now
housed.[37] The possibility that MS 176 was written in Waterford must
therefore be allowed.

In view of their actual and potential Waterford origins, it is
tempting to link MSS 176, 177, 181 and 182 together as a group,
perhaps the nucleus of a collection in existence before O'Byrne's
time. In this regard, Kilrossanty may well prove to be a focus of
attention. Manuscript 181 appears to have been written there. We
have just seen that Tomás Ó hIceadha, the scribe of MS 176, was
associated with the area in at least one of his productions.

---

[33] *NLI Cat.* ix (1986) 18 (G 388). I believe that Ó hIceadha's handwriting also
occurs in the second part of Harvard MS Ir. 3, containing an incomplete copy of the
tale *Ceisniomh Inghine Guil* and a section of Aonghus Ó Dálaigh's verse satire on
the tribes of Ireland, *Muintir Fhiodhnach na mionn*. The first part of the Harvard
manuscript is by Tomás Ó Briein of 'An Gleann Bán', probably Glenbane in the
barony of Clanwilliam, Co. Tipperary, scribe of RIA MS 24 D 35 (*RIA Cat.*, 3605-7),
UCC Ir. MS 95 and part of Belfast Public Library Ir. MS 7 (for which see B. Ó
Buachalla, *Clár na lámhscríbhinní Gaeilge i Leabharlann Phoiblí Bhéal Feirste*
(Baile Átha Cliath 1962) 5), thus furnishing another link, however indirect, between
Ó hIceadha and Tipperary. A note on Ó Briein will appear in Dr P. de Brún's
ongoing publication of the list of 'The Irish Society's Bible Teachers, 1818-27', in a
forthcoming issue of *Éigse*. A full description of Harvard MS Ir. 3 is included in the
work mentioned above, note 8.
[34] For the influence of the transfer of his clerical patron, Fr Patrick Wall, to
various assignments in Waterford on Ó hIceadha's involvement with the same
county, as well as a general sketch of the scribe himself see [Rev. P. Power],
Waterford and S.E. Ire. Arch. Soc. Jn. 1 (1895) 186-8. In *Éigse* 13 (1969) 11-25 Rev.
Pádraig Ó Súilleabháin edited one of a number of sermons from RIA MS 23 H 17
which he believed Ó hIceadha translated from English, but which are not correctly
attributed in *RIA Cat.*, 2864-5.
[35] M. Dillon, C. Mooney, OFM, P. de Brún, *Catalogue of Irish manuscripts in
the Franciscan library, Killiney* (Dublin 1969) 76-7 (MS A 38).
[36] Now in St John's College, Waterford, for which see Ó Fiannachta,
Leabharlanna na cléire I, 1-2, 6-9, 9-10, 33-4, 40-41 (MSS 1, 6, 7, 27, 31).
[37] In addition to the items mentioned in the last note, see *ibid.*, 2-5, 17, 26-8,
30-32 (MSS 2-4, 14, 21-2, 24-5).

Ballykerogue, the address of William Gough, probably a former owner of MS 177, is in Kilrossanty parish;[38] cf. the reference to the neighbouring [Catholic] parish of Abbeyside in the same page of this manuscript. The intermediary in MS 177's transmission southwards from the barony of Upperthird might conceivably have been the scribe Nioclás Ó Fuartháin, part compiler of UCC Ir. MS 40, written in the same Ballykerogue in the years 1837-8.[39] A discussion of the Waterford scribal network similar to Dr Breandán Ó Conchúir's account of the Cork literary milieu[40] will probably help ascertain the likelihood of such interrelationships between the documents.

Limerick: Of the remaining manuscripts, some definitely and others possibly also originated in the province of Munster. Taking the sources in sequence, ties with the Limerick area may be considered first. No place of writing is given for MS 175 (a) – (b). I have not been able to identify Tomás Ó Síothcháin, scribe of part (a), the manuscript's main section. Domhnall Ó Síothcháin, compiler of a portion of 175 (b) and presumably a relative of Tomás, may be the Daniel Sheahan who provided the nationalist politician William Smith O'Brien (1803-1864) with a number of Gaelic codices, many of them the work of the Co. Limerick scribe Séamus Ó Caoindealbháin.[41] In this connection it is interesting to note an association of Ó Caoindealbháin's with Seán Ó hÁinle, who wrote the main part of MS 178 in Gort Brien, Co. Limerick, in the years

[38] Power. *Place-names*, 149.
[39] This manuscript is described in Dr Breandán Ó Conchúir's forthcoming *Clár lámhscríbhinní Gaeilge Choláiste Ollscoile Chorcaí: cnuasach Uí Mhurchú*.
[40] For this work see below, note 47.
[41] For Sheahan, O'Brien and Ó Caoindealbháin see B. Ó Madagáin, *An Ghaeilge i Luimneach* (Baile Átha Cliath 1974) 78-84; for Sheahan see also P. de Brún, M. Herbert, *Catalogue of Irish manuscripts in Cambridge libraries* (Cambridge 1986) xxviii n. 205.
    I believe Ó Caoindealbháin's signature in English (James Quinlivan) also occurs in a note in p. 68 *i* (inverted) of UCC Ir. MS 176 (MS A of Thomas Canon Wall's Gaelic manuscript collection, on long-term loan from Laurel Hill convent, Limerick). The manuscript is a composite one, including portions by the scribes John Sheahan (pp. 45-57) and Donnchadh Ó Caoindealbháin (pp. 58-90), together with legal notices referring to William O'Brien of Highmount, Co. Limerick (between pp. 1 and 10). In view of the appearance of the surnames Ó Caoindealbháin. Sheahan and O'Brien in an early nineteenth-century Limerick – north Cork context in the document, a full study of this and the other items in the Wall collection may well shed further light on the Wisconsin codices discussed here.

1832-37.[42] Ó hÁinle was apparently a native of Co. Clare who had settled in Limerick by the early 1820s.[43] In 1824 he was criticised for allegedly misrepresenting a resident of west Limerick to the authorities as a supporter of the seditious Rockite movement.[44] It seems that Ó Caoindealbháin was the chief source of information which led to the composition of this forceful censure.[45] The work demonstrates an element of xenophobia with its insistence on Ó hÁinle's Clare origins and connections.[46] The place of writing and date of MS 178 suggest that Ó hÁinle did not suffer consequences sufficiently adverse as a result of the satire to cause him to leave Limerick county.

Cork: Connections with Co. Cork come next in order. Tadhg Mac Aogáin, scribe of MS 180, is to be identified by his handwriting with the person of the same name responsible for part of RIA MS 24 A 34, a verse anthology. He is believed to have had links with the Cork area.[47] Manuscript 183 also has Cork associations. Two former owners were from the county. John Long, a native of Curriglas[48] and subsequently a Wisconsin resident, bequeathed the document to the celebrated political activist Jeremiah O'Donovan Rossa

---

[42] I have not been able to identify Ioseph Ua Croimín, scribe of MS 178 (a).

[43] See Ó Madagáin (note 41), 94, for an account of Ó hÁinle, and also P. de Brún, *Éigse* 21 (1986) 129-30.

[44] Studies of the Rockite disorder include S. Ó Muireadhaigh, 'Buachaillí na Carraige, 1820-25', *Galvia* 9 (1962) 4-13; J. S. Donnelly, Jnr, 'Pastorini and Captain Rock: millenarianism and sectarianism in the Rockite movement of 1821-4', in S. Clarke and J. S. Donnelly (ed.), *Irish peasants: violence and political unrest* (Manchester 1983) 102-139; F. Whooley, 'The Rockite movement in north Cork 1820-25' (MA thesis, UCC 1986).

[45] Pádraig Ó Fiannachta has edited the text of the satire in *An barántas* I (Má Nuad 1978) 50-54. For the literary scene in which the work was composed, together with a treatment of Ó Caoindealbháin's participation in this, see P. de Brún, 'Forógra do Ghaelaibh 1824', *Studia Hibernica* 12 (1972) 142-66, especially p. 149.

[46] The composition describes Ó hÁinle as a 'donán diomách, ó imeallaibh Cláir' (Ó Fiannachta, 51 lines 21-2).

[47] Breandán Ó Conchúir has suggested this in *Scríobhaithe Chorcaí* (Baile Átha Cliath 1982) 17.

[48] The toponym's form in the manuscript may represent Curraglass, of which there are four instances in east and west Cork baronies. Orrery and Kilmore (1), Kinnatalloon (2) and Bantry (1), or alternatively Curryglass, of which there is one in the barony of Bear, and one in the barony of Orrery and Kilmore. See *General alphabetical index to the townlands, towns, parishes, and baronies of Ireland* (Dublin 1861) 349, 351.

(1831-1915), originally from Rosscarbery in west Cork.[49] O'Donovan Rossa lived in the United States from 1871 to 1894. While he was mainly prominent in the American public domain as a supporter of Irish nationalist causes, he also became involved with personalities in the Irish language movement.[50] Rossa and Long may have encountered each other in that way. I have not been able to determine the identity of the manuscript's scribe, Donnchadh Ó Cochláin. In view of the fact that he was also a versifier, he may be the poet Donncha Ó Cochláin, a handful of whose compositions survive in post-Famine sources.[51]

Uncertain: A number of problems surround MS 179, the last item to be considered. I have not succeeded in identifying the scribe. There are reasons for thinking that he could have been of northern origin. His surname might represent a form of the family name Mac Mathghamhna (MacMahon). While the surname is found in various parts of the country, its connections with Co. Monaghan are well established.[52] Although admittedly circumstantial, other testimony appears to support associations with more northerly parts of Ireland. Manuscript 179 may be the source of, or at least related to, the version of the tale 'Eachtra Chléirigh na gCroiceann' in BL MS Egerton 156.[53] Following its copy of the saga, the latter codex includes a colophon, part of which, 'Ar na sgríobha le Domhnall ac Mothanna an 6ᵃ lá don Bhealtuine 1603' (f. 52 b), virtually repeats the information given at the conclusion of MS 179 (p. 108). The compiler of Egerton 156 was the nineteenth-century scribe James MacQuigge, who appears to have had a northern background. In a note to another of MacQuigge's writings, the well-known scholar and antiquarian James Hardiman (1782-1855) suggested that he was from Co. Mayo. In the same brief biographical sketch, Hardiman stated that 'He copied from other books, but composed and

---

[49] For his biography see S. Ó Luing, *Ó Donnabháin Rosa* I-II (Baile Átha Cliath 1969-79)

[50] Ó hAnnracháin (note 6), 19.

[51] P. de Brún, *Clár lámhscríbhinní Gaeilge Choláiste Ollscoile Chorcaí: cnuasach Thorna* I (Baile Átha Cliath 1967) 137-8 (MS T li, pp. 32-6), 235 (MS T 12, pp. 60-72).

[52] E. MacLysaght, *Irish families* (Dublin 1957) 217-18.

[53] *BM Cat.* II, 366-8, contains a description of the manuscript.

14   INTRODUCTION

translated some'.[54] A number of manuscripts showing instances of MacQuigge's influence survive. Among their interesting features is the fact that they seem mainly to be works of midlands or northern provenance.[55] The choice of MS 179 as the probable source of the Egerton 156 saga may reflect this preference of MacQuigge's for documents of a more northerly orientation.

The exact date of MS 179 is also uncertain. The colophon referred to above states that it was completed in 1603, a detail confirmed by the reading in MacQuigge's copy. The realisation that MacQuigge showed an inclination to work with somewhat older codices may lend further support to the idea of its relatively early age.[56] However, the document also includes an element of eighteenth-century verse, composed by the Munster poet Seán Ó Tuama. In this connection, one wonders whether 1603 might not be an error for a later year, for instance 1803. In light of the foregoing considerations, the date of MacQuigge's transcription, 7 May 1816,[57] provides the only incontrovertible *terminus ante quem* for MS 179.

---

[54] These remarks occur in RIA MS 24 K 45, p. 6, *RIA Cat.*, 3132. The note also includes criticism of MacQuigge's character ('He was a forward ignorant man') and apostasy ('He was a Catholic, but recanted, & became a Methodist'), which Hardiman freely, and often more trenchantly, expressed elsewhere (e.g. RIA MS 23 K 33, p. 73, *RIA Cat.*, 1688; BL MS Egerton 156, f. 1, *BM Cat.* II, 366). The account concludes with the statement that MacQuigge 'was selected to superintend, or rather *Edit* !!, an edition of the Protestant Bible in *Irish*, but in English character, printed in thick 8.° Dublin, about 1825, a task for which he was utterly incompetent. But they could get no other' (cf. *BM Cat.* II, 366). For McQuigge's association with the Irish Bible cf. P. de Brún, *Éigse* 19 (1983) 306 n. 166. C. Túinléigh, 'Séamas Ó hArgadáin (1782-1855)', *Galvia* 3 (1956) 47-62, outlines Hardiman's own career.

[55] Thus MacQuigge provided an interleaved translation of and other additions to BL MS Egerton 662, a document compiled by the Dublin-based scribe Muiris Ó Gormáin in 1770 (*BM Cat.* II, 364). He also annotated BL MS Egerton 164, written for the most part by Pádraig Ó Doibhlin of Co. Meath in 1726-7 (*ibid.*, 345).

[56] In addition to the date of the items mentioned in the last note, MacQuigge copied and translated part of the fifteenth-century MSS BL Add. 11,809 (*BM Cat.* II, 545-51) and NLI G 9 (*NLI Cat.* i (1967) 58, ii (1961) 45-8), containing religious tracts in Irish.

[57] *BM Cat.* II, 368.

This survey suggests that the Dillon Collection is a valuable source of knowledge about various facets of the Irish tradition. The four UWM compilations associated with the Waterford area demonstrate the strength of the county's scribal heritage. They illustrate the need for an in-depth examination of this topic. The Limerick and Cork codices supplement information in Professor Breandán Ó Madagáin's and Dr Breandán Ó Conchúir's important studies of those regions.[58] The case of MS 179 is less definite, but at least it shows that the career of its colourful former owner, James MacQuigge, merits greater attention. The recent history of these manuscripts highlights the assiduous cultivation of Gaelic culture in late nineteenth-century New York. It points to the existence of substantial evidence for the writing of this untold story.[59] The overview presented here may assist further discussion of the issues raised.

The volumes themselves are described in accordance with the practice of recent Irish manuscript descriptions.[60] The catalogue's main objective is, arguably, to facilitate the edition of individual texts. Scholarship of the latter type will ultimately determine the quality of the compositions recorded in the collection.

---

[58] For these works see above, notes 41 and 47 respectively.

[59] In 'Irish Studies theses 1987/88', *Newsletter of School of Celtic Studies* (Dublin Institute for Advanced Studies) 2 (1988) 24-9, p. 24, Finola Flanagan is reported to be preparing an M.Litt. thesis for Trinity College, Dublin, on 'Mícheál Ó Lócháin agus *An Gaodhal*', a personality and a newspaper both closely associated with the New York Gaelic scene.

[60] See P. de Brún, 'The cataloguing of Irish manuscripts', *ibid.* 1 (1987) 33-4, for a succint review of present trends and future developments required in this area.

CATALOGUE

175

Battle sagas

19th cent. Paper. 18.5 × 14.5 cm (cover), 18.5 × 15 cm (leaves). Pp. 396 + 2, (a) main MS, now paginated in pencil (pp. 33-41 bearing scribal pagination 3-11, omitting 8; incomplete and inaccurate pencilled pagination between pp. 1 and 387 ignored); (b) loose leaf, 29 × 18 cm, folded horizontally twice to fit in (a), now paginated 1-2. Scribes: (1) principal scribe, *Thomas O Sheacan* (*Thomas Sheahan*) (pp. 7, 16, 42 etc.), 1817 (p. 91), 1818 (p. 376), 1823 ((b) p. 1), mentioning exemplar on p. 7; (2) lower half of (b) p. 2, *Dobhnal O Sgheacan* (*Danl Shehan*), 1833.

Bound in goat stitched over boards. Kept in phase box inside buckram covers. Collation obscured in binding, but MS apparently gathered in twelves and eights. Ruled in dry point, with catchwords on versos. Pages of (a) watermarked 1814; acid staining (due to use of newspaper cuttings as bookmarks) on pp. 22-3, 120-21, 301-2, 335-6, 341-2, 359-60; occasional burn marks throughout. Pp. 1-2 torn with slight loss of text. Burn marks and frayed edges in (b).

'Rare Books Dept / MS – 175', p. 1, upper margin (in pencil). Newspaper cuttings used as bookmarks between pp. 22 and 23 (from *New York Times* 30 Oct. 1916), 301 and 302 (from *The Fatherland*, undated), and 335 and 336 (unidentified and undated).

(a)

p.
1. 'CATH CHLÚAN TARRABH an so et maorgacht priobh cuarradh inte.' Beg. *Dó bhí búanacht Lochulanach có mór suin air Éirin nár mheidir leó fuillíng leis. . . .* Ends (p. 7) *Et ní diomhaoin do Ruiridhe O Conochubhir sin namm sun ach aig a ngeárra aig guin as aig treann bhuala ná mór Lochlannach gón nar fagbhug aon ar laithir [laiti* cancelled] *diobh gann bas daómirt air.* 'Guirbh mhe sin Cath Clúanna Tarabh ar nó sgriobh le Thomas O. Sheacan fea mar do fúairis as luarr do louribh an puiríos as ni darimm go bhuil gó hiommlann ann. As a léothir úasil guíg cuimh Dia fa trocré do dheanam ar mánamh go flathás na ngrást Amenn'.

7 *i. File cliste fuinnte an eolus.* 1 q.

8. 'D'FHIANNAIBH EIRION ann so sios.' *Beg. Biodh a fhios agad a leaghtheor chardeamhail tar cheann go nabraid mórán nách raibh Fionn inna Fianna Eirean ann.* . . . Ends (p. 16) *An deichmhádh coinighil ní gaibhthi aoin fear ionnta múna ttugadh na móde fá bheith dilios úiraimach dFíonn et dó bhris Diarmuid mac Duinna an comhnil.* 'Deire leis na comhnil fea mar do fuarrais aoid as guig ar suin Thomhas a leothar'.

16 *m. Mamhar gac fáig as a dána do dhrithimh riomh.* 1 st. Foll. by scribal colophon: 'Uirrispa uolis feánara na lúoichta a ta son labhar so sgríofa'.

17. 'Stholo Thol na go foil [*sic*].' *Do dhóir gán dearmud táisge gach stóar.* 8 stt. Foll. (p. 19 *i*) by scribal colophon: 'A theaimh fhiar guíg lé thainm an té do sgríog an lio stho mar fuar Maidinn Doúinnig as laigh suirre as traithnonna dobhuinn núir fuir sthe sin an gobha crío gheal do bhío sthal an. aulann'.

20. Finionn O Sgainnil. *Mo léan mar threásgarag gan tapa gan feasimh.* 5 stt. 'Air Eirin.'

23. 'CATH CNUCHA an so ma [*sic*] leannas.' *Beg. Déirig iomuig forúmad éad mór idír cúridhe et ceann fimmidhe na thEirinn.* . . . Ends (p. 29) *guir leir ghuin guir lann ghearadur gó nabaduch fior calama fir Leatha Caoinn guir leirguin et guir lann dibiríog leo iad eile.*

30. Blank.

31. 'CAITH GÁBHRA an so már leainns nár ndiag.' *Beg. Dó bí innion mhor mhreagh mhallrosgach mháorga machanta ag Cairbre mhac Córmach mhic Art.* . . . Ends (pp. 41-2) ⁊ *an san tánig an meid do mhár don / bhFeinn os cionn Usguir* ⁊ *nior fhann aon dé ar bith san gcaith acht iad uile a caoíne Usgur.* 'Foirceann leis an aistáidh sin do reir ma [*sic*] fuaramar e. Deire don meid sin liomsa Thomas Ó Sheacan'.

42. 'UACHT USGUIR an so.' Prose introduction: *Och así aonghuin Charbre do sgár mise leamm chairdibh na raibh aig laimh ar bith mo thitim acht ag sleag Charbre le nar tarragearach mo thitim* ⁊ *aig an millacht trí bhrisi an chúníol do bhí adir sin* ⁊ *Macon gan comhrac a gcuinibh a cheile go brach. – Ar aon chás air bith.* Foll. by verse beg. *Slan uim do fleabhaibh saora.* 22 lines.

43. 'TOIRIOCHT CEALLACHÁN CHAISIL ann só.' *Beg. Trachtfuim air ann fhlathús Lochlanach air nó Muimhineachibh et án módh air*

ar hionnarbhúg ⅂ air ár léir sgriosach as an Mumhuinn ead. . . .
Ends (p. 91) *gúir mhor an truadh búirrthioch ná nógláoch aig túirguínt na dtréan chuiruidhe a córpiobh a ceille gúir brísioc air ná Lochlaníg an is nár an áon air laithir diobh gán léirsgríos.* 'Guir bé sin Torighiocht Cheallachan Caisiol air ná sgríob lé Tomas O Stheachán agus guíg oruim a léigthoir 1817'.

92. Blank.

93. 'CATH CLÚAN TARRAMH ann so.' Beg. *Do bhí búanach Lochúanach* [sic] *co mór sin ar Eirinn nar mhéidir leo fuillíng na cuir suis leis. . . .* Ends (p. 120) *Bó dhoigh linn nar mho dle donn locht do bi sin ccath na donn locht do bhi no raoire.* 'Air nó sgriobh le Thomás .O. Sheacann gobha an tara la dhon tara maoí 1818 1818' [sic].

120 *m. A leaghtheor gasda do labharan caoin Gaodhalge.* 1 st.

120 *i. Teanga do bhuime a bhille meabharuig se.* 1 st. Foll. by: 'Eir son Déa guíg orm a leothair lé duiracht'.

121. 'CAITH CHNOCHA an so mur leanus.' Beg. *Deirig iomúigh forumad mor idir curidhe na thErin már nar mhaith le Mogh Néad mac Dérg mic Déirgthine na le cláinnimh Derigthine . . . Conn .cead. catha do bheith aig gabhail ceánnuis Eirinn. . . .* Ends (p. 187 *m) Do gháibh Conn ár sin ceánnas as comharbhus tri gcóige dÉirinn mur do bhi cóige Ulla cóige lamhdheárg Laighíonn as coige comhaluinn Connocht. Deiridh.* Scribal colophons: 'Thomas .O. Stheachann fear dilis an lobhar' (p. 135 *i*); 'Thomas .O. Stheacan fear an labhair' (p. 178).

188-96. Blank.

197. 'Triallamáoid D'IONNSAÍDHE MHUÍGHE LÉANA.' Beg. *Ionnsaíghe Mhuíghe Léanna sonn dár attóirchar Eogan Taidhleach. . . .* Ends (pp. 294-5) *Gidheadh tángadar go hÉirin a ccíon bhliadhna le mórann allumhrach as do gabhádar cuan an Easdára a gcríociobh Chonnocht amhail. / is léir don star re a raidhtar Caith Mhuighe Muchrúime as bimid anóis ag triall ann.* 'Sgrifo le Tho(m) Ó .A.A.lann' [?]. Scribal signature, 'Thomas Sheahan Smith', p. 213 *i*.

295. 'CAITH MUIGE MUCHRAIMHE ann so.' Beg. *Airdrigh crodha cruithmamha ceartbhreathach do ghaibh ardcheánas na hEireann go bfreasabhra dar bhainm Art Ollcosantach áirdghniomhach . . . .* Ends (p. 376) *An sin do rin Oilliol a*

úaghacht sé sin flaithius Múmhan do bheith ag Cormac ar feadh a réidh as a bheith ag Fiacha tar eis ar feadh a réidh féin mar sín do ghréas an flaithius do bheith idir óighríobh Eoghan as Córmach. 'Gón .e. sin Chaith Mhaigh Múcrúime as úagacht Oilliol Oluim um oighreacht Mumhan. Deire'. Foll. by scribal colophon: 'An triú lá do Ghéire eis an teacha 1818 ┐ sirim guigh an leothra le am amuanúin ar suin Dea amén'.

377. Traditions about Art mac Cuinn, Cormac mac Airt and Cairbre Lifeachair. Beg. *Seibhearas feartine + ocht mbliadhna a rioghacht an domhain a ccómhaimsir re hArt mac Cuínn as Aurelius seacht mbliadhna....* Ends (p. 387) *gur fógair caith ortha a nGabhra ionnar thuit se fein as ionnar cúireadh dearg ar ná Feine ionnus na rabhadar an Fheann ar bunn asíonn a leith amhail is lear dón star da ngoirthear Caith Gabhra as dó gheófar a dteásach an leamhar so .i. D.E.R.E.* Foll. by scribal colophon: 'Uairim ar gach leothar úasal guígh cuimh Dea fa tróchrai do dheanamh ar mánam as ge mór luaichti an leamhar so ni le am thuill si tharlág acht le thirispa eoluis'.

388-95. Blank.

(b)

1. NA HAOINTE ÓRGA. Beg. *Gibe duinne throisgfeas na haointe seo air arán ┐ air uisge, air aon phríonn amhain san ló gon oidhche, ┐ adéarfas na húrnaighthe seo sios an sgach Aoine....* 29 lines.
1 *i. Gaib garb muin chughad go heasga.* 2 stt., first giving date 1823, noted in calculation.
2. *Gaib mo leaghsgeal a leighthór bhínn.* 1 st. First two lines repeated in hand of second scribe.
2 *m.* Headlines and pen trials: (a) *A righ do cuilan gac rod a riogan og mait.* 1 line. (b) *An fa denter an Aoine na thrusca do* [. . .] *rer er lan do an* [. . .]. 1 line (repeated). (c) *Ar madon inne a tastal dom le gar na nean is me macnumh lom air gac.* 1 line (given four times). (d) *An uabhair is minnic me cuiripuc claonntac.* 9 lines. Line 1 repeated three times at conclusion of text. Foll. (p. 2 *i*) by scribal colophon: 'Dobhnal O Sgheacan gomh an 2 la do Abran an so mbin diocmh Criost air tiarna an tan sin .m.ccc.xxxiii 1833 Danl Shehan'.

176

Trí Biorghaoithe an Bháis

19th cent. Paper. 20.5 × 13.5 (cover), 19.5 × 12.5 (leaves). Pp. 304, now numbered in pencil (incomplete and inaccurate scribal pagination ignored), with one binder's leaf at front and stubs of two binder's leaves at back. In the hand of *Tomás Ó hIceadha*, 1851-2 (pp. 1, 304).
Bound in half-calf on marbled boards, with faded gilt-tooled ornamental raised bands on spine. Front cover detached; spine loose. Collation uncertain. Substantial loss of text due to cutting away of leaves between pp. 289 and 304. Ruled in pencil and dry point, with catchwords and running headings throughout most of MS. Upper and lower edges occasionally trimmed, resulting in loss of text and page numbers. Ink staining on lower outer margins to p. 79 'Rare Books Dept MS – 176', p. 1, upper margin (in pencil). Pencilled scribbling, front binder's leaf, recto. Pencilled annotation of text (interlinear glosses, marginal notes etc.) throughout, in non-scribal hand, possibly that of Mícheál Ó Broin. Bookmark (fragment of unidentified newspaper) between pp. 284 and 285.

p.
1. 'TRÍ BIOR-GAITHE AN BHÁIS le Seathrún Céitinn. D.D. sagart purráiste Thiobruid. A.Ch. 1620. Air na ath-sgríobhadh anois. 1851.' Beg. *A n-ainm an Athar, .⁊ an Mhic, .⁊ an Spiorad Naoimh. Amen. An Chéad Alt. Do h-órduigheadh dona daoinibh uile bás dfaghail aon uair amhain do réir Phóil. easb. etc.* ... Ends (p. 304 *i*) *Agus guidhmíd Dia uilechomhachtach, le sinn uile do stiuradh tar gach bearnuin baoghail, ⁊ tar gach guais. go ccriochnuighthear an rioth úd linn, ⁊ go ngabhthar Flaithios Dé linn, mur a ffagham. ⁊ mur a ffeudfam, an geall comh-liongadh, atá dá thuar, ⁊ dá thuilliomh linn. do ghreamughadh, .⁊ a bheith inár seilbh go síorruighe Amen.* 'Abrán 30, 1852'.

177

Sermon; lexicon; verse

18th cent. Paper. 20 × 17 cm. Pp. 160, in two sections, (a) pp. 28, with scribal pagination 5-32; (b) pp. 132, with scribal pagination 1-[2], 3-34, 37-89, 92-4, 277-80, 283-90, 311-[322], 323-40 [for gaps in text see below], and one binder's leaf at either end. Scribe: *Labhrás Ó Horáin* (*Ó Thorráin, Ó Fúartháin*) ((a) p. 31, (b) p. 1 etc.), (a) in Baile Uí Chnaimhín [par. Mothel, Co. Waterford], 1762 (p. 31); (b) in Baile Uí Chnámhín and Portlách [Co. Waterford], 1762 (p. 1), 1766 (p. 316) and 1782 (p. [2]).

Bound in half-calf, with blue paper on boards; spine detached from back cover. Kept in phase box inside buckram cover. Collation uncertain. Leaves in section (a) pp. 5-27 and section (b) pp. 278-9 mounted on paper hinges; pp. 283-90 of (b) now loose; upper half of pp. [321-2] torn away. Ruled in ink and dry point, with catchwords. Text in section (b) pp. 3-94 in columns with running heading. Pages stained, especially in section (b) pp. 285 ff. Undated watermark present.

'William Gough Ballykerogue / August the 14th. 1866' ('7' faintly in ink after second '6') and 'Parish of Abbeyside' (in pencil), recto of front binder's leaf; 'Rare Books / MS – 177' on verso, otherwise covered with scribbling in ink. Cutting from unidentified newspaper (possibly *New York Times*; entries refer to New York for years 1915-16) between pp. 16 and 17 of (a). Back binder's leaf, verso (in pencil, inverted): (a) *Dear Erin thy flowers are faded and gone.* 14 lines. 'The Shamrock.' (b) Signature 'John [*pencil*] Gough [*ink*] Goff [*pencil*]'. Retracing of text in blue crayon throughout MS, frequently obscuring original punctuation and lengthmarks. Marginal and interlinear glosses in blue crayon, and also in pencil, in same hand as annotations in MS 176.

For the connection between this manuscript and NLI G 311 see Introduction, note 28.

(a)

p.
5. [SEANMÓIR AOINE AN CHÉASTA.] Beg. acephalous *Do leig sé as,*
ag rádh o Dhia o Dhia a tria na ngrás créad an fáth air tréigis no
air shéanuis me. . . . Ends (p. 31) *furtaigh* ⁊ *saor sinn ó nár*
nguais, et treoruigh sinn chum an bheatha mharthanach. an ní
go ttugadh Dia dhíbhse, et damhsa. An anim an Athar .⁊ *an*
Mhic .⁊ *an Spiorad Naomh.* 'Ag sin Seannmhóir Aoíne an
Chéasda. Iar na prescrit le St. Dáibhí o Labhán. Tugach gach aon
eisdeas no léaghfeas í beannacht air anam an sgríbhneóra do
sgríobh ann so í eadhon Labhrás Ó Horáin Maighistir bocht
Sgoile a mBaile Uí Chnaimhín an Uachtar Tíre a bPuéracha an
19 lá do mhí na Bealltainne an san mbliadhain dáois an
Tighearna Íosa Críost mar as léir ann so. 1762. no MDCCLXII.
Moladh do Íosa Críost. Amen. FINIT'. Foll. by scribal colophon:
'GO MOLTAR AINIM AN TIGHEARNA LE NA CHRÉATÚIRIDH GO
HUILE ANOIS GO BRÁTH ⁊ LE SAOGHAL NA SAOGHAL AMEN a
Thighearna'.
32. *Is truagh gan mise sa ríghbhean míle léig ó chúan.* 6 stt.
'Abhrán.'

(b)

1. Title-page: 'Ag so DICTIONARÍ NO FOCLÓIR NO SANASÁN NÚA
Ionna míníghthear cruadh fhocail na Gaoidheilge, ar na
Gaoidheilge [*sic*], ar na sgríobhadh ar úrd aibghittire air ttúis le
brathair bocht túata d'órd S. Prionsías .i. Mícheal Ó Cléire, a
cColáisde na mBrathair nÉirionnach a Labhán, agus air na chur
a cclódh maille re húghdarás 1643.// Do Sgríobhadh anois go
núa é san leabhrán so le Labhrás O Thorráin, a mBaile Uí
Chnámhín, an Uachtor Tíre a bPuéaracha, chum a shochar féin,
⁊ cum glóire Dé ⁊ leas anma ⁊ tairbhadh a chomhairsan an 18
la don Mhárta san mblíadhain daois an Tighearna 1762.
MDCCLXII. Deo Gratias.// MOLADH DO ÍOSA CRÍOST. Amen.//
LABHRÁS Ó FÚARTHÁIN A BPORTLÁCH ANNO DOMINI 1782'.
[2]. Later title-page: 'AG SO DICTIONARÍ NO FOCLÓIR, NO
SANASÁN NÚA. Ionna míníghthear crúadhfhocail na
Gaoidheilge. Ar na sgríobhadh air úrd aibgitire air ttúis, le

brathair bocht túata dórd S.Pronsías .i. Mícheal Ó Cléire a
cColáiste na mBrathar Néirionnach a Lobhán Et air na chor a
gclódh maille re hughdarás 1643. Air na Sgríobhadh amach
maille le Labhrás Ó Fúartháin a bPortlách an 29 lá fithchiod don
Abrán an San mblíadhain daoís an Tighearna 1782. an lá is
fúaire do chonairc me ó rughadh me san am cceadna do
bhlíadhain.// GLÓIR DO DHÍA GO BIOTHBHÚAN. AMEN.// Aig
so Dictionári no Foclóir nó Sanasán Núa, ioná mínighthear
crúaidh hocail na Gáoilgé, air na Sgríobh amác re Labhras. Ó,
Fuairtháin 1782.// Labhrás .Ó. Fuarthain'.
3. [SANASÁN NUA.] Beg. *Al .i. ard no cnoc*. Gap in text due to
missing leaf between pp. 34 and 37; no loss of text between pp.
89 and 92 despite pagination. Incomplete, as catchword
soichearnsa, following last entry *sognaigh .i. soghnaoieach .i.
gniomh maith* (p. 94 *i*), indicates.
277. [EACHTRA AN MHADRA MHAOIL.] Beg. acephalous *bheatha
uile duine is mó comhachta ná é, ⊓ an úaimh dhorcha is ainm
don ionad na ndeáchaidh as so.* . . . Gap in text due to loss of pp.
281-2. Breaks off with p. 290 ⊓ *tug bean eile bo táire na í, .i.
inghean Rígh na beagna ⊓ ata dun a leithimeall na crichesi, ⊓
an dún diamhair is ainm dhó.*
311. [Dáibhidh Mac Gearailt. *A mhic na páirte, táimse 'ad agall.*]
Beg. acephalous *Tar gach rían do thriall a Sagsaibh. c.* 68 lines
+ 3 ('Ceangal') stt. Foll. (p. 314) by scribal colophon: 'AR NA
SGRÍOBH LE LABHRÁS Ó FÚARTHÁIN AN SAN MBLÍADHAIN
D'AOÍS AN TIGHEARNA 1766'.
315. *Súd bean rith soir an Thebe.* 19 lines.
316. *Smúinigh páis Chríost a ccáil Ríogh na ngrás dáonacht.* 9 lines.
Foll by scribal colophon: 'DEIRE LEIS AN MÉID SIN. An
ceathramhadh lá don Meithiobh, a bPortlách an Úachtor Tíre a
bPaoracha, a gContáe Phortláirge, le Labhrás Ó Fúartháin an
San mblíadhain d'aois an Tighearna Íosa CRÍOST mar as follus
annso 1766. BUIDHEACHUS DO DHIA'.
317. An tAthair Padraig Ó Bruin. *Tóigfaigh sé atuirse is brón díbh.*
59 lines.
320. *A gabháil dam do mhullach an cchím* [?]. *c.* 5 stt. Ends
incomplete (p. [322] *m*).
[322] *i.* Donchadh Mór Ó Dála. *Ní thug an tAthair dá ainglibh dísle.*
c. 89 stt. Breaks off with p. 340.

178

Battle sagas

19th cent. Paper. 19 × 16 cm (cover), 18 × 15 cm (leaves). Pp. 274, (a) front endpapers, pp. [i-xx]; (b) main manuscript, pp. [ii] + 232 (with scribal pagination 1-21, 23-30, 32-50, 52-70, 72-150, 152-225, 228-238; loss of text between pp. 225 and 228 only) + 1 (now numbered 239); 20 blank unnumbered endpapers at back, with two binder's leaves at either end. Scribes: (1) main scribe, *Seaghan Ó Hainle* (*John Hanly*), of Goirtinn Briain (Gorth Brien) [par. Caherconlish, Co. Limerick], 1832-6 (pp. 38, 75, 100, 156, 175, 216). (2) front endpapers, *Ioseph Ua Croimín* (p. [i]).

Bound in half goat and patterned cloth on boards. On spine, gilt-tooled ornamental headbands and stamping, together with 'IRISH / MANUSCRIP' [*sic*] in gold lettering. Collation uncertain. Ruled in pencil and dry point, with catchwords and occasional ornamental capitals. Tears in section (a) pp. [i-ii] and section (b) pp. 1-23 (lower margins) have been repaired. Name 'Cowan' in watermark in front and back endpapers, with pages of main MS watermarked 1827. Page-numbers and text clipped at outer edges of main MS. Some staining throughout.

Notes and jottings: (a) inside front cover. 'A/3/IH' and 'Dáithi Ua Caoímh / 134 Sráid Aonta / Brúchlinnd Theas / HF', both in pencil (the second erased but recoverable). (b) first binder's leaf at front, recto. 'Air' (pencil; Irish script), 'Is liomsa Micheál Ua Broin / an leabhar so / an 30adh lá de mhí na Fabhra / 1905 / Eabhrac Nuadh'. (c) section (a) p. [i], upper margin. 'Rare Book Dept / MS − 178' (pencil). (d) ibid. p. [xv]. 'gus na dig / agus na da atamaoid anais a cuisle / mo croidhe be so an cead lá dar saoithibh com luaithe / Agus mairionn dá raibh lathair a Phadruig achd mise.' [main MS:] (e) [i]. 'Shemus.' (f) 38, lower margin. 'Domhnal Magnaer.' Scribbling in pencil, p. 41 *i*. Loose printed leaf (folded horizontally in centre) with running heading 'Gems of Poetry' included as bookmark.

(a)

p.

[i]. Title page: 'INNS AN Leabhar so atá trachda air Na mór-cathaibh thug CÚCULLAINN, mar aon le Cath Chnucha, Oidhe Clann Uisneach ⁊ Caith Clúana Tairbh, ⁊ c. Ioseph Ua Croimín'.

[ii]. Blank.

[iii]. 'Tuirreamh na hÉirion le Seaghan Ua Connaill Easbog Árd Fearta 1650.' *An uair a smuainím air saoitibh na h-Éirionn*. 20½ stt. Breaks off with p. [vii].

[viii-xx]. Blank, except for item in p. [xv] noted above.

(b)

[i]. Blank.

[ii]. Table of Contents, foll. by scribal colophon: 'Ná tuig ad taigne a leaghthóir gur sgéala bréagach ná fiansgéal failigheachta tá annsa leabhar. Ni headh go deimhin dearbhtha óir atá laoide agus leitir lé gach nidh atá ann ⁊ gach (ugh)dar ás barrántamhuil cum a bheith fírinneach ⁊ da brigh sin baistimse mur ainim air an leabhar seo [. . .]a binn na fírinne'.

1. 'OILEAMHUINN CHONGULOINN, annso.' Beg. *Conguloinn mac Siubaltaig flaith do mhacaibh cloinne Rúgraídhe do shliocht Ír mhic Mílidh*. . . . Ends (p. 38) *i*) ⁊ *ní raimh an aonfheacht aig aon rígh do riogaibh an domhain riamh laochra bfearr ná na laochra sin air a ttugthaoi curadha na Craoibhe Ruadh amhuil is follus ionnarr ndiaigh*. 'Gonadh é sin Oileamhuin Ch. Ch. go nuige sin an mhéid fuaireasa di. Foirchean. Finished by me John Hanly'.

39. CÓMHRAG FIRDIAIGH AGUS CUCHULLAINN. Beg. *Do bhadur cheithre hollchoige Éirionn daon aonta a anaighhidh* [sic] *Chóige Ulladh*. . . . Ends (p. 75 *i*) with conclusion of Cú Chulainn's poem *Cluithe gáire cómhrac chách* and note: 'FINIT. This transaction Happened about 38 years Before the Birth of Christ according to the best authority I could find – Finished by me John Hanly of Gorth Brien this 6th Day of January 1832'.

76. Blank.

77. OIDHIDH CHONNLAOICC MHIC CUCHULLAINN. Beg. *Dala na mna toiriche dfag Cucullain a ccríochaibh na Gréige an tan*

tainig foirchionn naoi miosa. . . . Ends (p. 100 *i*) with conclusion of Cú Chulainn's poem *Truadh sin a aonfhir Aoife*. 'This event Happened about 50 years before the Birth of Christ. Finished this 24 Day of February 1832. Air na sgriobh re Seaghan Ó Hainle a nGoirtinn Briain is aitchim guídhe gach léagthóra cum leas anma agus cuirp dfáighil'.

101. 'CAITH CNOCA, sonn.' Beg. *Do bhadur Laighnig leath air leath gan raith gan rígh ró cónach déis Chathaoir Moir mhic Feidhlime*. . . . Ends (p. 156 *i*) with conclusion of Ciothruadh's poem *Calma do chaithréim a Cuinn*. 'The Reader is to Observe that this Battle was fought in the year of Christ 155. Finished by me John Hanly this 28th Day of February 1836. Críoch mar fuaireas'.

157. 'CAITH CHLUANA TARBH annso.' Beg. *A.D. 1022. Do ghaibh Brian Boirbhe mac Cinéide . . . ríoghacht Éirionn da bhliaghain déag*. . . . Ends (p. 175 *m*) *Ionnus gurab e sin Caith Chluana Tairibh ⁊ mur du thuit Brian Boirbhe mac Cinneide.* 'Annsa mbliaguinn daois Chríost 1014 tugadh an caith réimhráighte an Aoinne ria Caisg. Finished by me John Hanly this 16 Day of March 1836. Críoch mur fúairios. Gaibh mo leithsgial a léaghthóir ionnmhuinn má tá locht san obair seo óir is se olcus mo pheann easba meabhrach is me bheith neamhthuigsionnach fá ndearra dham a dhéanamh. John Hanly'.

176. 'BRISLEACH MUIGHE MUIRTHEIMHNE annso.' Beg. *Feacht naon dá ttangadar Ullaidh go hEamhuinn Macha go súbhach soimheanmnach*. . . . Ends (pp. 215-16) *Ann sin do sgaoileadur fir Éirionn dá ccóigeadhaibh agus dá bfearrannaibh ⁊ ró órduigheadur dá ccurraidhe agus dá ccaithmhílidh a bhfághbháil / dá niomchoiméad air eagla Chonnaill cCeárrnaig do breith orrtha.* 'Gurab i sin Breisleach Muíghe Muirtheimhne ⁊ mur do thuit C.C. go nuige sin. This great Battle was fought about the year of the world 3960 or 40 years before the birth of Christ according to the best authority I could find. Foircheann mur fuairios le Seaghan Ó Hainle a nGoirtaoin Briain an chéad lá don Miosa December aois Chriost an tan san .i. míle hocht gcéad agus seacht mbiaghna [*sic*] déag air fhithchid. Aicim guídhe an léaghthóra mur aon leis an lucht eisteachta trocaire do thabhairt dam anam an tan bhus bás dham. Gaibh mo leithsgial a

leaghthóir má ta locht annsa nobair so oir do chuirios síos é mur fuairios'.

216 *i. A shuarcfhir bheoltais do mhór shliocht Shreonuil.* 2 stt.

217. Blank.

218. 'OIDHEACHT CHLAINNE HUISNEACH SONN.' *Rígh uasal óirdhearc árrdchómhachtach ró gaibh ceannus choige Ulladh dárrab comhainnim Conchúbhar mac Fachtna Fathaig. . . .* Ends (p. 238 *i*) with conclusion of Deirdre's poem *As fada an lá gan clann Uisneach.*

[239]. Scribal note: 'Ni'l agus ní raibh riamh aon bhunudhas a tuilleas ár sgrudhughadh nios fearr na an Eaglais Caitliochach Romhanach'.

179

Tales; Ossianic verse

19th cent. [?]. Paper. 15 × 8.5 cm (cover), 15.5 × 9 cm (leaves). Pp. 108, now numbered in pencil. Scribe: *Domhnall ac Mothánna (Domhnall ac Taig)* (pp. 74, 108); date 6 May 1603 supplied, p. 108.

Bound in paper, with front cover loose from binding. Kept in phase box inside buckram covers. Collation uncertain. Pp. 12-21, 24-5 on paper hinges, with many leaves detached from binding. Paper stock of pp. 25-36 and 49-70 distinct from remainder of MS, containing faint undated watermark and vertical chain lines. No discontinuity of text between different paper stocks. Textual sequence shows order of pp. 74-6 to be 76, 75, 73, 74. Ruled in dry point and pencil with occasional catchwords. Manuscript stained throughout, with ink faded in parts, especially in pp. 11-12.

'Rare Books / MS / 179', p. 1 (in pencil). Pencilled sketches of human profile inside front and back covers and in p. 1.

For relationship of this manuscript to BL MS Egerton 156 see Introduction,

p.

1. Mainly blank: see above.

2. 'A COMPENDIOUS IRISH GRAMMAR or an Introduction to the Irish Language.' Beg. *Of the Irish alphabet Commonly Called*

Aibgitir na Gaolgeadli. Ends incomplete (p. 10 *i*) with account of the *Five Epthongs.*

7. Satirical prose passage. Beg. *Runruntac cnaoiste caca caoimhtheach cearthach caoic a gceastaibh punncumhla.* . . . 16 lines.

11. Litany. Beg. *A Conghamh na cCriostaighthe. c.* 35 lines.

13. 'Siabhradh sit ⁊ INEIRGE MÍC NA MIODHCOMHAIRLE agus an dán air am fann do cumadh le Cearball [. . .] Dalaigh ris a raitear Aisde Cearbhaill.' Beg. *Mar cualaidh sibhsi ni misde dibh a fhiafraighe diomh.* Verse interspersed with prose. Ends (p. 68) with conclusion of verse *Sguirim fein feasda dom thaisdiol gan bhrigh gan aird* 'F.I.N.I.T'.

48 *m* (inserted in previous item). 'Baisteadh Oisín.' *Padricc Oisin is fada do shuann.* 1 q.

69-70. Blank.

71. ['Barántas an Choiligh.'] *Contae Luimnid mar aon le mor cuard Eirean go huile. Ag so gearan geartuirseach an Atar Seagan Ui Lieidinn .i. sagart suaimneach . . . do latar Seagann Ui Thuamadh an grínn.* . . . 10 lines (incomplete).

76. *Cnoc an Ár an cnoc so shuas.* 19 qq. Foll. (p. 74 *i*) by scribal colophon: 'Domhnall ac Taig do sgriobhadh e so ⁊ beanacht ar anam ⁊ abaramaoid uile amen'. For order of leaves see introductory remarks, above.

77. *Ni threigfuinnsi mac De bhi.* 49½ qq.

86. *Gealluidhimse fein gan bhreig is mfeidhirdhe ort.* 1 st.

87. Blank.

88. 'Ag so sios na coinghil oile do cuir le Faon as grada gaisge fa heigean do gac aon do gabhail suil gabhthaoi a bFianuigheacht etc.' Beg. *An cead coingiol ni gabthaoi neac san bFein a Mordhail Uisnig na an aoneac Tailltean.* . . . 36 lines.

89. [EACHTRA CHLÉIRIGH NA GCROICEANN.] Here entitled 'An Reithe Riogha – .i. An Righ ⁊.' Beg. *Righ uasal oirdheirc ceillighe ceartbhriarac do gaibh flathas . . . ar Erin . . . dar ba comhainm Conall Ceannbhagar mac Feariosa mic Conall Gulban.* . . . Ends (p. 108) *Gluaisios Aongus go sugach comheanmnac ⁊ dag righ Eirean go dubhac domheanamnac. Ni cian go bhfuar Righ Laigean bas tre cumha a mhna fein.* 'Ar na sgriobha le Domhnall ac Mothána an 6 la don Bhealtaine 1603 FINIT'.

180

Accentual verse

19th cent. Paper. 15.5 × 10 cm. Pp. 218, with scribal numeration 1-32, [33-4] (blank, unnumbered), 65-102, [103-4] (stub; leaf torn out), 105-250. Scribe: Timothy Egan (*Tadhg mac Aogain*), 1836-7 (pp. 136, 239). Unbound; kept in phase box inside buckram covers. Largely gathered in fours. Pp. 1-4 detached from binding. Ruled in pencil and dry point, with catchwords and ornamental capitals bearing zoomorphic designs. Edges of leaves frayed and stained. Inner margins of pp. 3-4 torn with loss of text.

'Rare Books / MS 180', p. 1, upper margin (in pencil). Fragment of note in pencil, p. [104] *i*, in handwriting similar to that in pencil in MS 176 and in crayon and pencil in MS 177. Texts commencing on pp. 27, 99, 139, 144, 162, 177, have A.D. dates and in some cases annotations in different ink and non-scribal hand (possibly that of pencilled note).

p.
1. Uilliam mac Cairteain an Dúna. *Mairg do chualaidh marbh a tuairisg faoi leacaibh a ttuam.* 18 stt. 'Air bhás Mhaire Ní Chormuic Spáinnicc san mblian 1724.'

9 *i*. Seaghan Ua Murchughadh. *As cúmha sus creach don Mhuinn go bhfeas.* 16 stt. 'Air bhás Uilliam mac Cairteáin November 1724.'

17 *i*. Micheal Ó Longáin. *Aig taisteall bhíos le taoíbh na Sionna maidionn aoíbhinn mhín gan chuisne.* 34 + 1 ('Ceangal') stt. 'Air bhás Mhichíl mhac Pártalán Uí Cháoimh.'

27. Seaghan Ó Túama. *Ata sáod ghalar nimhe am ghéarghoin go huile.* 5 + 1 ('Ceangal') stt. 'Beó Chaoíne Seaghain Chlaraicc A.D. 1790.'

29 *m*. idem. *Go déaghnach is Pheabus fá neól.* 7 + 1 ('Feart Laoí') stt. 'Marbhchaoíne an fhir cheadna.'

[33-4]. Blank.

65. 'Bean na ttrí mbó.' *Go réig a bhean na ttrí mbo.* 10 qq.

67 *i*. Seághan Cúndun. *A Uí Chaoimh mo thrí mhile slán leat*. 47 stt.

78 *i*. Dáibhi Cúndún. *Is búartha an cás so a ttárlaidh Éire*. 77½ stt.

99. Muiris mac Dáibhi Dhuibh mhic Gearailt. *Ait liom stéad sgiamhach sgafánta*. 11 qq. 'Air rogha ⁊ díth na mban. A.D. 1612.' Bottom of p. 101 and all of p. 102 blank.

105. Tadhg mac Díarmada Uí Dhála. *Atá grádh nách admhuím orm*. 7 qq. 'A.D. 1618.'

106 *i*. 'Confessio mar leanas.' *Ní cheilim na bearta do charus an aoís móige*. 7 + 1 ('Ceangal') stt.

109. *A shlait leabhair na ccíoch mbláth*. 6 qq.

110 *m*. *Ailne aicfhionn nách faiciom*. 6 qq. + 1 st.

112. *Mór idir na haimseachaibh* [sic]. 71 qq.

127 *i*. *Sgéal air dhiamhar na suirghe*. 18 qq.

131 *i*. *Fir na Fódhla ar ndul déag*. 14 qq.

135. *A saogail dhiróil mar dhris*. 1 q.

135 *m*. *Mo cheithre rann duit a Dhonnchaidh*. 6 qq. Foll. (p. 136 *i*) by scribal colophon: 'Timothy Egan Feby. the 7 Anno Domini – 1836'.

137. Máoldomhna Ó Muiriosáin. *A mhna goiliom tre Ghlas Áir*. 8 qq. (incomplete).

139. Muiris Mhac Daibhi Dhuibh mhic Gearailt. *Gabh mo theagasg a mhic*. 9 qq. 'A.D. 1612.'

141. idem. *Gaibh mo theagasg a inghin fhíonn*. 12 qq. 'Dá inghin.'

144. 'Fearghal Mhac an Bhaird ⁊ é an Albuin.' *Beannocht úaim síar go hÉirinn*. 26 qq. 'Prob. A.D. 1600 – if identical with Fearghal Óg Mac an Bhaird.'

150. Uilliam Scot. *Ní molla gan mían dána*. 15 qq.

153. Muiris Mhac Daibhi Duibh mhic Gearailt. *Sguir dot shuiríghe a ógain fhinn*. 21 qq. 'A.D. 1612.'

158 *m*. *Gabhuim mo dheith rainn san rían*. 10 qq. + 5 stt.

161 *i*. *Fear gan dán aig déanamh dan*. 1 q.

162. Tadhg Úa Concubhair. *Do cleasaibh an tsáoghail shlím*. 7 qq. Note about poet (in non-scribal hand): 'Prob. A.D. 1650 if identical with Tadhg Ruadh Ua Ch——'.

163 *i*. 'An freagra ar sin.' *Trúagh a Thaidhg mur caoíntear leat*. 9 qq.

165. Daibhi Mhac Gearailt. *Mollacht don bhás bhrónach*. 21 qq.

170 *i*. *Focal os cionn focal*. 1 q.

171. Magamhuin Ó Hifirnáin. *A mheic na meábhraig eigse*. 13 qq.

174. *A bhean óg on a bhean óg.* 7 qq.
175 *m. Me Fear Día on me Fear Díai.* 10 qq.
177 *i.* Tadhg Dall Ua Huiginn. *Mairg fhéacas ar Innis Cuillionn.* 39 qq. 'A.D. 1610.'
186 *i.* 'Laoí Chnuic an Áir.' *Cnoch an Áir an cnoch so shíar.* 18 qq.
191 *i.* 'Laoí na Seilge.' *Lá dá raibh Fionn na bhfleadh.* 50½ qq.
204. 'Laoí an Deirg sonn.' *Daithreósuinn caithreim an fhir mhóir.* 59 qq.
217. 'Laoí an Duirnn sonn.' *Feis ardaisge tígh Teamhrach.* 31 qq.
223. 'Laoí Mháoghnuis mhic Rígh Lochlonn.' *A chleirig ud chanas an tpsalm.* 39 qq.
231 *i.* 'Caithréim Fhinn mhic Cúmhaill sonn.' *Dursan tuitim an teó óir.* 36 qq. Foll. (p. 239 *m*) by scribal colophon: 'Tadhg mac Aogain an ceáthru lá do Iúl agus an sa mblían d'aois Criost 1837'.
239 *i.* 'Cómhrac Mháoghnuis mac rígh Lochlann ris an bFeinn sonn.' *Leacht Ghoill do chráig mo chroídhe.* 33 qq.
246 *i. As na mná cíodh mór bhur ndóith.* 1 q.
247. 'Teacht Láighne Mhóir air an bhFéinn sonn.' *Lá dá rabhsain a nDún Baoí. c.* 18 qq. Breaks off incomplete with p. 250.

181

Sermon

19th cent. Paper. 21.5 × 17 cm. Pp. 18, numbered by scribe. Scribe: *Rev. John Meany* (no scribal signature; identified by handwriting and colophon, p. 18), Killrossenty, Co. Waterford (p. 18). No date of writing given.

Nine loose leaves, formerly folded vertically in centre, with cracks at fold. In poor state of preservation. Ruled in ink. Words 'MFG. Co.' in watermark.

'Rare Books / MS – 181', p. 1 (in pencil), with stamp in ink of Matthew E. Gleeson (twice).

p.
1. 'SEARMÓIN GAOIDILGE. Air charthanacht, no grádh na ccomharsan.' Beg. *Innsidhean ár Slánaightheoir duinn, anns an*

*soisgéal an lae a niumh, an dualgas is treise atá againn le
cóimhlíonadh.* ... Ends (p. 18 *i*) ... *bheanacht atáim-si aig
iarraidh dhibhse agus dom féin, tré ár d-Tighearna Iosa Criost.
Amen.* Foll. by colophon in unidentified hand: 'Sermon preached
by Rev. John Meany. Parish Priest of Kilrossenty in the united
dioceses of Waterford and Lismore'.

182

Catechism

19th cent. Paper. 17 × 11 cm. Pp. 28, now numbered in pencil.
Scribe: *Riocard Paor*, Waterford, 1860 (p. 1).

Bound in paper wrappers from which the leaves have come
loose. Housed in pocket binder. Single gathering, shown by title-
page to be fragment of larger item. Ruled in ink and pencil, with
occasional catchwords. Tear in pp. 7-8 *i* repaired.

'Michl. O Byrne', p. 1, upper margin (in pencil). 'Rare Books /
MS – 182', p. 3, upper margin.

p.
1. Title-page: 'An / Teagasg Criostuighe,/ Agus / Úrnaidhe na
   Mainne,/ Agus / Na Trathnona,/ Air na sgríobhadh,/ le Riocard
   Paor./ a bPortlurgadh,/ 1860'.
2. Blank.
3. 'An Ainim an Athar, agus an Mhic, agus an Spioraid Naoimh,
   Amen. Urnuidhe roimh an Teagasg Críostuighe.' Beg. *Tabhair
   grasa dhuinn, a Thíghearna.* ... 6 lines.
3 *m*. [AN TEAGASC CRÍOSTAIGHE.] Beg. *An Chéad Cheacht / Do
   chruithughádh, agus do chríth an duine.* ... Breaks off with p. 28
   in Twelfth Lesson of Part Two.

183

Prose; accentual verse

19th cent. Paper. 14 × 9.5 cm (cover), 15.5 × 10 cm (leaves). Pp.
160, now numbered in pencil. Scribe: *Donchadh Dl O Cochláin*
(*Donnchadh dl.*[=O] *Cochlain*) (pp. 141, 146); scribe's initials, *Duir
Óir Coll*, p. 131 (cf. p. 116). Compiled between 1823 (p. 43) and 1826
(p. 146).
Bound in leather (or possibly vellum) over boards, the latter
consisting of compressed printed sheets reporting British
parliamentary proceedings. Kept in phase box inside buckram
covers. Collation uncertain. Pp. 1-2 detached from binding. Ruled in
dry point. Heavy dark oil-stain throughout, leaving salt traces on
many leaves and obscuring text from mid-page to inner margins.
Text hidden at inner margins due to binding. Loss of text and page-
numbers on upper and lower edges from trimming. Watermarks
unclear in stain.
Notes and jottings: (a) 3, upper outer margin (in pencil). 'Rare
Books MS – 183.' (b) 8. 'Louisa Hunt August the 11th 1836 Commd.
[. . .] ship well Riged will [. . .] the [. . .] M(ay) 18 [. . .] illous [. . .].'
c. 6 lines. (c) 115. '[. . .] John Long [. . .]ll is my [. . .] and with t[. . .].'
c. 4 lines. (d) 115, outer margin (trans.). 'John Long of Curriglas
Cork, dying in Waterville Wis. in 1892. Willed this book to me.
Rossa 7/10/93.' (e) 131. '1826. Diarmaid O'Donnobháin Rossa Oct
7/93.'
Included with MS is a leaf, 15 × 14 cm, bearing transcript in
unidentified hand of note in p. 115 marg. (above), foll. by words
'(O'Donavan Rossa)'.

p.
1. [EACHTRA AN MHADRA MHAOIL.] Beg. acephalous *na tonnaibh*
⁊ *na bruachaibh dorcha dithchéilídhe gur chlos fá na críochaibh
ba cóimneasa dhóibh. . . .* Breaks off with p. 7 . . . ⁊ *Allustrum
iongantach mainm* ⁊ *as inghean do righ na [. . .] Niamh
Nuadhchrothach* ⁊ *do rugh si ceathrar.*
8. See above.

9. Eoghan Ui Suilliabháin. *Is atuirseach gear mo sgeal foríor.* 10 stt., with English translation *A doleful tale I'll relate to thee.* 'Cct an [. . .] bheith pe an Erin í.'

12 *m.* idem. *Sin agaibh mo theasdas air bheatha gach réice.* 8 stt. 'Dob fhearr léigion dóibh.' Foll. (p. 15 *i*) by: 'Der(e) mar fuairis'.

16. idem. *Am leabain areir trí am neul do dhearcusa.* 5 stt. 'Teaghlach Jackson.'

22. idem. *Dá méigs me cheapach dúanta le fúamint is laoighthe.* 5 + 1 ('Ceangal') stt. 'Moladh Mháire inghean Ghiobúin.'

27 *m.* idem. *Mo chás mo chaoidh mo cheasna an fáth tug claoidhte an easba.* 9 stt. 'Seághan Ó Daoighir.'

32. idem. *A tasdiol na sléibhte dam sealad am aonar.* 8 stt. 'Seaghan Buídhe.'

36. idem. *Ceo draoigheachta a ccáim oidhthe do sheól me.* 9 stt. 'Ragairne an tSoighdiúra.' Foll (p. 40 *m*) by: 'Críoch de sin etc.'

40 *i.* idem. *A bhile gan chealg sa sheabhac don fhíorfhuil.* 20 stt. 'An tÁrachtach Sean.' Date 'January The 11th 1823' after st. 6 (p. 43 *i*).

51. idem. *Dá ma aon me a ttuigsinn éifeacht do leighfeach mar Shésair.* 5 stt. 'Moladh Mná.' Foll. (p. 53 *m*) by: 'Deire leis sin etc.'

53 *i.* *Nuin sa dó go dlúth na déig is cúpla caogad gléasda a ccoir.* 1 st. 'A hainim.'

54. Eoghan Ui Suilliabháin. *Cois na Siurach maidin drúchta is me támhach lag faon.* 11 stt. 'An Clár Bog Déal.' Foll. (p. 57 *m*) by: 'Crioch de sin mar fúairis etc.' .

57 *i.* idem. *Mo leun [le] luadh agus matuirse is ní féur do bhuinn air theasgannaibh.* 7 stt. 'An Spealadóir.' Foll. (p. 61 *i*) by: 'Crioch de sin etc.' Scribal colophon, p. 57 *i*: 'Ar na sgríobh an 13 lá don bhlíadhain núadh aois an Tíghearna 1823'.

61 *i.* 'Easgaine Eogain Ui Suilliobháin air mnaoi dheimigh fhocal do ghlaca le tuistiun do chionn boinn do chuir fa [stocaidhe] dho.' *Easmailt is ár gach lá ort go dúbalta. c.* 10 stt. Foll. (p. 64 *i*) by: 'Crioch de sin mar fuarus'.

65. idem. 'Bharantas Dhonnchadh Í Nunáin.' Beg. *Conntae Chorcaidhe mar aon le mór chúaird na hÉirionn go huile le hEógan Ó Suilliobháin.* . . . 41 lines (prose), with verse text, beg. (p. 67 *i*) *Whereas dáitibh aon dam láthair anáe gan tlás air bhrigh móide.* 40 + 3 ('Ceangal') lines.

70 *i.* idem. 'Bharántas an Hata.' Beg. *Aig so ordúgha fuinneamhuil feidhimlaidir fiochmhur.* . . . 10 lines (prose), with verse text, beg. *Eigse is suaga Shleibhe Lúachra eistig linne seal.* 64 lines. Foll. (p. 75 *i*) by: 'Crioch etc.'

76. idem. *Cois abhuinn dam am aonur a déaghnamh mo mharbhna.* 8 stt. Foll (p. 78 *m*) by: 'Crioch de sin'.

78 *m.* Aogán Ó Rathaile. *Gile na gile do chonnarc air slíghe an uaignis.* 7 + 1 ('Ceangal') stt. 'Gile na Gile.' Foll. (p. 80) by: 'Críoch de sin mar fuairios etc.'

80. 'Fear gan ainim.' *Trath araoir 's me tnáite a bpeinn air fán an tsaoghail 's gan duine am gh*[. . .]. 6 stt. Foll. (p. 83 *m*) by: 'Crioch de sin etc.'

83 *m.* 'Fear gan ainim.' *One morning fair condoling I roved by the river Bride.* 7 stt., alternating with 7 stt. of Irish, beg. *Maidean aorach aoibhinn cois Bríde dam seal go dubhach.* Foll. (p. 87 *i*) by: 'Crioch etc.'

88. 'Chum an Athair Uilliam úasail ghle mhianaicc da Norra.' *A bhile gan chadam gan chalg gan chlaoin chéime.* 8 stt. Foll (p. 90) by: 'Crioch de sin etc.'

90 *m.* 'Duine gan ainim.' *Maidion aeghrach dam am aonar, aig taisdioll taobh re Teabhair síos.* 9 + 1('Ceangal') stt. Foll. (p. 93) by: 'Crioch etc.'

93 *m.* Tádhg Gaodhalach [Ó Súilleabháin]. *Araoir is me am aonar cois taoibh leasa an Ghaortha.* 7 stt. *i*

97. 'Fear gan ainim.' *Am aonar seal a siúbhal bhíos a ttúis oidhche a ngaortha ceó.* 8 stt. 'Air fonn Móirinn Ní Chuillionnáin.'

99 *i. Muin is nuin duir is coll is t.* 1 st.

100. 'When you go into the chapel say the following words in Irish.' *Go mbeanuíghthear duitse Iosa Criost go mbeanuighthear duitse a theampcholl na Trionoide.* . . . 8 lines.

100 *i.* 'When leaving the chapel say the following words viz.' *Slan agad a chruis a chrann an duilleabhuir ghluis.* . . . 11 lines.

102. An Mangaire Súgach. *A shagairt a rún ná diúlta a mbliadhna pis.* 4 stt.

103 *m.* Seághan Ó Tuama. *Cidh fada mo chsiubhal annsna triuchaibh íasachta.* 2 stt.

104 *m.* An Sagart. *As earbhúr fíonntar duinn le cían an phis.* 2 stt.

105. An Manngaire Sugach. *A bhuinnáin shultmhar a shiollaire shúgaicc shéimh.* 6 stt.

107. An Manngaire. *A shagairt na páirte is cásmhar mise le ceart.* 1 st. 'Do shlat an Athair Muiris Líghe.'

108. An tAthair Uilliam mac Gearailt. *A chuisle chaoin na féithe dfíor sgoith chruinn na néigse.* 8 + 1 ('Ceangal') stt.

111 *m*. Eamonn O Báire. *Sa shagairt ghil na míne sa Ghearaltaicc don fhiorfhuil.* 8 + 1 ('Ceangal') stt.

116. 'Duir Óir Coll cct.' *Araoir is me taisdiol cois abhan am aonar.* 7 + 1 ('Ceangal') stt.

121. Dómhnald Ó Bríain. *A leógain na náran féuc tráitheamhuil ad thímpeall.* 6 stt.

125 *m*. Eógan Ó Suilliobháin. *Slán et daithchiod le ceangal ceart díograis.* 8 stt. 'Do fheinn.' Foll. (p. 131) by scribal colophon: 'Air na sgriobh le Duir Óir Coll Novr. 6 A.D. MDCCCXXVI'.

132. Eoghan O Suilliobháin. *Gach teinnios is galar mairg is gnás is créim.* 4 stt. Foll. (p. 133) by: 'Críoch etc.'

133 *m*. Díarmuid mac Dómhnaill mhic Fíghnín Chaoil. *Is léun liom leagadh na bhflatha is na bhfíorúaisle.* 14 stt. Foll. (p. 138) by: 'Crioch etc.'

138. An tAthair Uilliam Inglis. *Mar chéile gabhaimse leatsa a bhuime Íosa.* 11 stt. Foll. (p. 141 *i*) by: 'Crioch. Donchadh Dl O Cochláin'.

142. 'Moladh Anaicc le hEoghan O Suilliobhain. an tan do fiafraighaidh san Bhlárnain de a bfeacadh sé tír na lucht aitribh a ccomheas don tír sin et da lucht áitribh.' *Cidh seoladh le tréimhse me a straeghriocht do shíor.* 7 stt. Foll. (p. 146 *m*) by: 'Crioch. (Airna) sgríobh liomsa Donnchadh dl. Cochlain an 18mad don miosa November aois ar tTíghiorna an tan san MDCCCXXVI. Íarrim do beannacht [. . .]'. Last two lines of colophon illegible.

147. *A Criostaighthe seanaig se a chleasa.* 1 st.

147 *m*. Lexical note on word *iongabháil*, with explanations in English of its usage.

148. Aindrías Mac Cruitín. *As fada me bpeinn ám chéill air fághan.* 6 stt. 'Do inghin Uí Dhonchadha .i. Séafra.'

154. 'Irish Words with their meaning in English.' Beg. *Dearnad 'a Flea'.* Includes letters D-E, T.

INDEX TO FIRST LINES OF VERSE

A shagairt na páirte, is cásmhar mise le ceart (An Mangaire). **183**, 107.
A shaoghail dhearóil mar dhris. **180**, 135.
As arbhar fionntar dúinn le cian an phis. **183**, 104 (part of series).
A shlait leabhair na gcíoch mbláth. **180**, 109.
A shuaircfhir bheoltais de mhórshliocht Shreonaill. **178** (b), 216 *i*.
As na mná ciodh mór bhur ndóigh. **180**, 246.
Atá, see *Tá*.
A Uí Chaoimh, mo thrí mhíle slán leat (Seán Cundún). **180**, 67.

Beannacht uaim siar go hÉirinn (Fearghal Mac an Bhaird). **180**, 144.

Ceo draíochta i gcoim oíche do sheol mé (Eoghan Ruadh Ó Súilleabháin). **183**, 36.
Ciodh fada mo shiúl insna triúchaibh iasachta (Seán Ó Tuama). **183**, 103 (part of series).
Ciodh seoladh le tréimhse mé ag straeireacht do shíor (Eoghan Ó Súilleabháin). **183**, 142.
Cnoc an Áir an cnoc-so thiar [al. *thuas*]. **179**, 76; **180**, 186.
Cois abhann dom im aonar ag déanamh mo mharbhna (Eoghan Ruadh Ó Súilleabháin). **183**, 76.
Cois na Siúire maidin drúchta is mé támhach lag faon (Eoghan Ó Súilleabháin). **183**, 54.

Dámadh aon mé i dtuigsin éifeacht (Eoghan Ruadh Ó Súilleabháin). **183**, 51.
Dámadh éigs mé cheapfadh duanta le fuaimint is laoithe (Eoghan Ruadh Ó Súilleabháin). **183**, 22.
Dear Erin, thy flowers are faded and gone. **177**, back binder's leaf, verso.
De chleasaibh an tsaoghail shlim (Tadhg Ó Conchubhair). **180**, 162.
D'aithreosainn caithréim an fhir mhóir. **180**, 204.
Do-gheobhair gan dearmad taisce gach seoid. **175** (a), 17.
Dursan tuitim an t-eo óir. **180**, 231.

Easmailt is ár gach lá ort go dúbalta (Eoghan Ó Súilleabháin). **183**, 61.

Fear gan dán ag déanamh dán. **180**, 161.
Feis ardtaisge tighe Teamhrach. **180**, 217.
File cliste fuinte in eolas. **175** (a), 7.

Fir na Fódla iar ndul d'éag. **180**, 131.
Focal os cionn focal. **180**, 170.

Gabhaim mo dheich rainn san rian. **180**, 158.
Gabh garbhmhuin chugat go héasca. **175** (b) 1.
Gabh mo leithscéal, a léitheoir bhinn. **175** (b), 2.
Gabh mo theagasc, a inghin fhinn (Muiris mac Dáibhí Dhuibh Mhic Gearailt). **180**, 141.
Gabh mo theagasc, a mhic (Muiris mac Dáibhí Dhuibh Mhic Gearailt). **180**, 139.
Gach tinneas is galar is mairg is gnás is créim (Eoghan Ó Súilleabháin). **183**, 132.
Geallaimse féin gan bhréig is m'oidhrí ort. **179**, 86.
Gile na gile do chonnarc ar slí in uaigneas (Aogán Ó Rathaille). **183**, 78.
Go déanach is Phoebus fá neol. (Seán Ó Tuama). **180**, 29.
Go réidh, a bhean na dtrí mbó. **180**, 65.

Im aonar seal ag siúl bhíos. **183**, 97.
Im leabain aréir trím néal do dhearcas-sa. (Eoghan Ruadh Ó Súilleabháin). **183**, 16.
In uabhar is minic mé coirpeach claontach. **175** (b), 2 m.
Is atuirseach géar mo scéal, faríor (Eoghan Ó Súilleabháin). **183**, 9.
Is buartha an cás so i dtarlaidh Éire (Dáibhí Cundún). **180**, 78 i.
Is cumha 's is creach don Mhumhain go bhfeas (Seán Ó Murchadha). **180**, 9.
Is fada mé i bpéin óm chéill ar fán (Aindrias Mac Cruitín). **183**, 148.
Is léan liom leagadh na bhflatha is na bhfíor-uaisle (Diarmaid mac Domhnaill mhic Fhinghin Chaoil). **183**, 133 m.
Is trua gan mise 's an rí-bhean míle léig ó chuan. **177** (a), 32.

Lá dá raibh Fionn na bhfleadh. **180**, 191.
Lá dá rabhsain i nDún Baoi. **180**, 247 (incomplete).
Leacht Ghoill do chráidh mo chroidhe. **180**, 239.

Maidean aerach aoibhinn cois Bríde dom seal go dubhach. **183**, 83 (with trans.).
Maidean aerach dom im aonar ag taisteal taobh le Teamhair síos. **183**, 90.
Mairg do chualaidh, marbh a tuairisc (Uilliam Mac Cairteáin an Dúna). **180**, 1.

Mairg fhéachas ar Inis Ceithleann (Tadhg Dall Ó hUiginn). **180**, 177.
Mallacht don bhás bhrónach (Dáibhí Mac Gearailt). **180**, 165.
Mar chéile gabhaimse leatsa, a bhuime Íosa (An tAthair Uilliam Inglis).
    183, 138.
Meabhair gach fáidh is a dtáinig do dhraoithibh riamh. **175** (a), 16 *m*.
Mé Fear Dia, ón mé Fear Dia. **180**, 175.
Mo chás, mo chaoi, mo cheasna (Eoghan Ruadh Ó Súilleabháin). **183**, 27.
Mo cheithre rann duit, a Dhonnchaidh. **180**, 135 *m*.
Mo léan le luadh 'gus m'atuirse (Eoghan Ruadh Ó Súilleabháin). **183**, 57.
Mo léan mar [do] treascradh gan tapa gan faoiseamh (Finghin
    Ó Scannaill). **175** (a), 20.
Mór idir na haimsearaibh. **180**, 112.
Muin is nuin, duir is coll is t. **183**, 99 *i*.

Ní cheilim na bearta do charas in aois m'óige. **180**, 106.
Ní moladh gan mian dána (Uilliam Scot). **180**, 150.
Ní thréigfinnse Mac Dé bhí. **179**, 77.
Ní thug an tAthair dá ainglibh dílse (Donnchadh Mór Ó Dálaigh).
    177 (b), 322.
Nuair (An uair).
An uair smaoinim ar shaoithibh na hÉireann (Seán Ó Conaill).
    178 (b), [iii] (incomplete).
Nuin 's a dó go dlúth 'na déidh (Eoghan Ruadh Ó Súilleabháin). **183**, 53.

One morning fair condoling I roved by the river Bride (trans.). **183**, 83 *m*.

Scéal ar dhiamhair na suirghe. **180**, 127.
Scoir dod shuirghe, a ógáin fhinn (Muiris mac Dáibhí Dhuibh Mhic
    Gearailt). **180**, 153.
Sin agaibh mo theastas ar bheatha gach réice (Eoghan Ó Súilleabháin).
    183, 12.
Slán is daichead le ceangal ceart díograis (Eoghan Ó Súilleabháin).
    183, 125.
Slán uaim do fhlaithibh saora. **175** (a), 42.
Smaoinigh páis Chríost i gcáil Ríogh na ngrás daonnacht. **177** (b), 316.
Súd bean rith soir don Thebe. **177** (b), 315.

Tá (Atá).
Atá grádh nach admhaim orm (Tadhg mac Diarmada Uí Dhálaigh).
180, 105.

Atá saighead-ghalar nimhe dom ghéarghoin go huile (Seán Ó Tuama).
180, 27.

Teanga do bhuime, a bhile, meabhraighse. **175** (a), 120.

Tógfaidh sé atuirse is brón díbh (An tAthair Pádraig Ó Broin).
177 (b), 317.

Tráth aréir 's mé tnáite i bpéin. **183**, 80.

Truagh, a Thaidhg, mar chaointear leat. **180**, 163 (reply).

Whereas d'áitigh aon dom láthair (Eoghan Ruadh Ó Súilleabháin).
183, 67.

GENERAL INDEX

[References preceded by 'p.' and 'n.' respectively are to pages and footnotes of the Introduction.]

Abbeyside (Co. Waterford). Placename, **177**, marg.; p. 11.
'Agallamh Oisín agus Phádraig', p. 8.
'Aiste Chearbhaill', see Siabhradh sídhe.
An, Na, The (definite and indefinite articles), see under following element.
Ancient Order of Hibernians. Wisconsin branch, n. 2.
Aointe Órga, Na h. 175 (b), 1.
'Árachtach Sean, An t.' 183, 40.
Ardfinnan (Co. Tipperary), p. 10.
Art mac Cuinn. Traditions about, **175** (a), 377.

Baile Uí Chnáimhín [al. Ballynevin] (par. Mothel, Co. Waterford). Place of writing, **177** (a), (b) [part]; pp. 8, 9.
'Baisteadh Oisín.' 179, 48.
Ballykerogue (Co. Waterford). Address of former owner, **177**, marg.; p. 11.
Bantry, barony (Co. Cork), n. 48.
['Barántas an Choiligh']. 179, 71 (incomplete).
'Barántas an Hata.' 183, 70
'Barántas Dhonnchaidh Uí Núnáin.' 183, 65.
Barron, Philip, pp. 6-7.
'Bean na dtrí mbó.' 180, 65.
Bear, barony (Co. Cork), n. 48.
Best, R. I., p. 4.
Bloomfield, Morton, n. 5.
Brisleach Muighe Muirtheimhne. 178 (b), 176.

Cairbre Lifeachair. Traditions about, **175** (a), 377.
'Caithréim Fhinn mhic Cumhaill.' 180, 231.
Carmody, Patrick. Manuscript transcriber, p. 7.
Casey, Fr Michael. Manuscript owner, p. 7.
Cath Chluana Tarbh. 175 (a), 1, 93; **178** (b), 157.
Cath Cnucha. 175 (a), 23, 121; **178** (b), 101.
Cath Gabhra. 175 (a), 31.
Cath Muighe Mucroimhe. 175 (a), 295.
Ceisniomh Inghine Guil, n. 33.
Céitinn, Seathrún, see Trí Biorghaoithe an Bháis.

Feir(r)itéar, Pádraig. Scribe, 19th cent., and owner, n. 7.
Fian. Conditions for membership of, **179**, 88. See also D'Fhiannaibh Éireann.
Folds, John S. Printer, n. 17.
Foren, Ml., see Ó Forranáin.

'Gile na gile.' **183**, 78.
Gleeson, Matthew E. Name in stamp, **181**, 1.
Glenbane [*al.* An Gleann Bán] (Co. Tipperary). Place of writing, n. 33.
Goirtín Briain [*al.* Gort Brien] (par. Caherconlish, Co. Limerick). Place of writing, **178**.
Gough [*al.* Goff], John. Signature, **177**, marg.
Gough, William. Former owner, **177**.
Graystown (near Killenaule, Co. Tipperary), p. 9.

Hanly, John, see Ó hÁinle.
Hardiman, James, p. 13.
Harvard University, pp. 3-4. Houghton Library, n. 8; Pusey Library, n. 10. See also Robinson, Fred Norris.
Heist, William, n. 5.
Highmount (Co. Limerick), n. 41.
Hyde, Douglas, n. 21.

Inglis, An tAthair Uilliam. Poem by, **183**, 138.
Innéirghe Mhic na Míchomhairle, see Siabhradh sídhe.
Ionsaighe Mhuighe Léana. 175 (a), 197.
Irish language. Vocabulary, **183**, 147 *m*, 154. See also Dictionarí.

Kilkenny, county. Scribal tradition, p. 8.
Killeen (Co. Waterford), p. 8.
Kilrossanty (Co. Waterford). Place of writing, **181**; pp. 6-7, 10-11.
Kinnatalloon, barony (Co. Cork), n. 48.

'Laoi an Deirg.' **180**, 204.
'Laoi an Duirn.' **180**, 217.
'Laoi Chnoic an Áir.' **180**, 186.
'Laoi Mhaghnais mhic Rígh Lochlann.' **180**, 223.
'Laoi na Seilge.' **180**, 191.
Lehmann, W. P., n. 5.
Líghe, An tAthair Muiris. Poem for, **183**, 107.
Limerick, city. Laurel Hill Convent, n. 41.

48 GENERAL INDEX

Limerick, county. Place of writing, pp. 11-12, 15. Places in, Goirtín Briain (Gort Brien) [par. Caherconlish], Highmount, Limerick city.

Lismore (Co. Waterford), p. 8.

Litany. 179, 11.

Long, John. Former owner, 183.

Louisa Hunt. Name of ship, 183, 8 marg.

Mac an Bhaird, Fearghal [Óg]. Poem by, 180, 144.

Mac Aogáin, Tadhg [al. Timothy Egan]. Scribe, 19th cent., 180; p. 12.

Mac Cairteáin, Uilliam an Dúna. Poem by, 180, 1; elegy on, 180, 9.

Mac Carthaigh, see Máire Ní Chormaic Spáinnigh.

Mac Cruitín, Aindrias. Poem by, 183, 148.

[Mac Domhnaill], see Seán Clárach.

Mac Gearailt, Dáibhí. Poems by, 177 (b), 311 (acephalous); 180, 165.

Mac Gearailt, Muiris mac Dáibhí Dhuibh. Poems by, 180, 99, 139, 141, 153. Poem to daughter of, 180, 141.

Mac Gearailt, An tAthair Uilliam. Poem by, 183, 108. Poem for, 183, 111 *m*.

Mac Giobúin, Máire *Ní Ghiobúin*. Poem for, 183, 22.

[Mac Mathghamhna] ('ac Mothánna'), Domhnall (ac Taig). Scribe, 17th or 19th cent [?], 179; pp. 13-14.

MacQuigge, James. Scribe, 19th cent., pp. 13-15.

Magnaer, Domhnal. Name occurs, 178, 38 marg.

Máire Ní Chormaic Spáinnigh [Mhic Cárthaigh]. Elegy on, 180, 1.

Mangaire Súgach, An [Aindrias Mac Craith]. Poems by, 183, 102, 105, 107.

Mayo, county, p. 13.

Meany, Rev. John [al. Seán Ó Maonaigh]. Scribe, 19th cent., 181; pp. 6-7.

Meany, Rev. P. Scribe, 19th cent., p. 8.

Meath, county, n. 55.

'Móirín Ní Chuilleanáin.' [Tune], 183, 97.

'Moladh Eanaigh.' 183, 142.

'Moladh Mháire Ní Ghiobúin.' 183, 22.

Monaghan, county, p. 13.

Na, An, The (definite and indefinite articles), see under following element.

New York [al. Eabhrac Nuadh]. Mentioned, 178 marg.; The Bronx, n. 7; Hamilton Place, p. 2; Irish Industries Depot (bookstore), 780 Lexington Avenue, Manhattan, p. 3; South Brooklyn, address of former owner, 178.